MOM EGG REVIEW

2019 Vol. 17

Half-Shell Press
New York

i

Mom Egg Review is an annual collection of poetry, fiction, creative prose, and art by and about mothers and motherhood.

www.momeggreview.com.

Front Cover Image: Megan Wynne

Mom Egg Review is a member of the Community of Literary Magazines and Presses.

This publication has been made possible, in part, by a grants program of the New York State Council on the Arts, a state arts agency, and the Community of Literary Magazines and Presses. *Mom Egg Review* is grateful for this generous support.

Mom Egg Review thanks The Motherhood Foundation, *The Mom Egg* founding publishers, Joy Rose and Mamapalooza, and founding editor Alana Ruben Free.

Mom Egg Review can be purchased directly from the press on our website, through online retailers, at select independent bookstores, and through EBSCO.

Contact *MER* at info@themomegg.com for info about discounts for quantity purchases and for classroom use.

ISBN: 978-0-9915107-5-7
(Half-Shell Press)

Mom Egg Review
Half-Shell Press
PO Box 9037
Bardonia, NY 10954

www.momeggreview.com
www.facebook.com/momeggreview
Twitter: @momeggreview
Contact: info@themomegg.com

MOM EGG REVIEW

Vol. 17 - 2019

Editor-in-Chief
Marjorie Tesser

Poetry Editors
Jennifer Martelli
Cindy Veach

Readers for Vol. 17
Jessie Bacho, Patrice Boyer Claeys, Becky Ellis, Elizabeth Lara, Carole Mertz,
Theta Pavis, Ana C.H. Silva, Judy Swann, Nancy Vona

Copy Editor
Patrice Boyer Claeys

EDITORS' NOTES

Welcome to *Mom Egg Review's* seventeenth annual issue. I've been editing the journal since 2007, and I've noticed how, in an annual collection, the work can reflect the tenor of the times. I've never felt it more strongly than with the current issue.

This has been a complicated year in a series of complicated years. Countries and factions seem increasingly at odds. Hate has flaunted its ugly face around the globe, having appeared to have been countenanced. Our physical environment teeters and we disagree about the dire nature of this and what to do about it. Injustice and inequality reveal their tenacity daily. And through it all, mothers work and nurture families, children, partners, elders, and friends, and do what they can to ameliorate, counter, or re-direct the world's trajectory in ways personal and political.

In a climate where polarities are becoming the default, the literary works in this collection admit of nuance, of multiplicities of stories and viewpoints. They pinpoint hypocrisy so it can be examined and unmasked. They recognize that both challenges and beauties exist. These thoughtful, angry, hopeful voices can give respite and can spur resolve.

A word about our cover. Megan Wynne's arresting image of a mother there-and-not illustrates children's constant and profound need for nurture, for presence. This year we've experienced the horror of families ripped apart due to a harsh immigration policy. The image recalls those events, as well as the other reasons mothers and children may be distanced, including poverty, incarceration, lack of governmental support of working parents' crucial needs for child and elder care, and a mother's own urge to sometimes separate, physically or emotionally.

We bring you this issue thanks to the work of many. We are grateful to our contributors of exceptional writing and art, to our readers of submissions, Jessie Bacho, Patrice Boyer Claeys, Becky Ellis, Elizabeth Lara, Carole Mertz, Theta Pavis, Ana C.H. Silva, Judy Swann, Nancy Vona, and to Patrice Boyer Claeys for copyediting. We are blessed with the thoughtful vision of Poetry Editors Jennifer Martelli and Cindy Veach, as we have been by that of outgoing editor, Jennifer Jean. We value the creative contributions of our *MER VOX* online quarterly editors, Editor-at-Large J.P. Howard, Gallery Editor Ana C.H. Silva, and *MER VOX* Editors Jennifer Martelli and Cindy Veach. We send bouquets of thanks to our book reviewers and literary collaborators. All of us are grateful to you, *MER's* readers, and hope you enjoy the work in this issue.

Marjorie Tesser
Editor-in-Chief

In her poem "Mama Said This is the Way to Make Happy Kids," Margie Shaheed gives us the recipe for fried green tomatoes: "heat oil in black cast iron skillet 'til it smokes/gently place slices in sizzling oil. . ." Think of all the aspects of a recipe: the balance of the savory, the sweet, the salty; the community of cooks; the danger of the hot stove; and most important, the recipe's longevity—how it becomes a story, created, then passed down. When Jennifer Jean, the brilliant former poetry editor for *MER* passed us the baton (the recipe box), we knew we had work to do: how would we blend the myriad voices and textures? Thankfully, we were blessed with teachers and sisters in poetry with whom we could share our thoughts and ideas. When we read Margie Shaheed's poems, we knew they were important. Each one belied its simplicity, confronting this country's history, its racism, its cruelty and violence. Her poems distilled the enormity of motherhood and the holy act of passing down love, trauma, survival…and food. Shortly after accepting her work, we learned that Margie Shaheed had died. Her strong voice stayed with us, and we are forever grateful that her family allowed us to publish her poems posthumously. They truly embody and crown the poetry in this issue of *MER*. As we began to order all this fine work, we could feel the movement of motherhood from the mythological to the actual: trials that occurred in the Bible were manifested at the maternity ward, at the daycare, and later as we said good-bye to our children and to our own mothers. The childhood Shaheed's poems describe is marked by poverty and bigotry and grapple with today's landscape. And the mother's love that works to make the children happy during the worst of times is there, too. In the end, we have Margie Shaheed's poems and those of all the other fine contributors to this issue as perfect ingredients to nourish us and connect us to the unique flavors of other communities and other times.

Jennifer Martelli and Cindy Veach
Poetry Editors

CONTENTS

POETRY

FICTION

CREATIVE PROSE

ART

MOM EGG REVIEW

Vol. 17 - 2019

POETRY

April Matisz

Margie Shaheed

What I Wish I Could've Done

if i had the words of a dictionary
in my pocket i would shake them out
onto the floor piece sentences together
to form language to tell you the mysteries
of a mother raising nine children alone

i would stockpile all of the synonyms, adjectives and verbs
for "there's not enough food" and "we have to move again"
in a raggedy white box with one thousand lit
sticks of dynamite erasing their charred tongues
from the human lexicon forever

The Hough Riots

it was 1966 mama told us hough avenue was on fire
ignited over a 'no water for niggers'
sign posted at a white owned bar
burn baby burn rang out for six days
to neighborhood an urban war zone
at night mama cut off the lights in the house
darkness forced us to whisper
gathering at the windowsill like baby ducks
we peeked out hoping to catch glimpses
of army tanks rolling down our street
mama made it clear whose side we were on
we were black folks fighting for our rights
i wanted us to win

Margie Shaheed

Mama Said This is the Way to Make Happy Kids

slice green tomatoes an inch thick
salt and black pepper to taste
shake slices in brown bag with yellow corn meal
remove one by one
heat oil in black cast iron skillet 'til it smokes
gently place slices in sizzling oil
turn when edges brown
brown other side
place slices on paper towel to drain
eat with hot sauce

Marietta Brill

Sarah's Binding: Her Story

— And Isaac spoke unto Abraham his father, and said: 'My father.' And he said: 'Here am I, my son.' And he said: 'Behold the fire and the wood; but where is the lamb for a burnt-offering?' Genesis 22.9

And when he took you for a hike to *commune with the spirits* we laughed like it was a joke;

You and I were still one thing then, complete as an Eden (In the albums: never me, just you, and me reflected in your eye, as witness, implicit);

You so cute, wrapped like a shawarma;

After four months bound, I admit there was relief at first;

Unlocked from your gaze, my eyes drifted to a shaft of dust, a spinning cosmos;

And in the mid-day tick I slept, dreaming lambs in a thicket;

I woke to wild flurries, an empty house, cleaned and cooked;

My breasts engorged like a goddess of destruction—I stalked the door for hours clutching knives and forks gleaming like lightening;

At dusk you both blew past me in an icy gust

Your father's eyes blurred from cold and too much smoke;

The fact of the day bled from his mouth;

A carrion lie circling;

I'm here, he said, here we are, it's okay—but I read the truth;

In your eye;

In the burnt curl of gristle on your sleeve: *Nothing will be the same;*

He took you;

And somehow, I let you go;

From that day on, I was redacted from the story.

Deborah Bacharach

Sarah Interviews Hagar for the Position, Maid Servant

Do you have any STDs, including herpes? HPV?
Date of last period? Average length of stay?
Your history of drugs.
Do you hum while you scrub? Do you bathe?

Describe a child-proofed room.
Your stance on discipline.

What do you do for croup?
How many pears have you canned this season?
How often do you smear tar on your slip?
How well do you wash it out?
Show me.

Do you shop at Walmart? Do you snarl like a camel?
Do you smoke?

Should a leader be feared? Your opinion of course.
When were you last slapped?
What do you do when you need to scream?

Learning disabilities?
Family history of heart disease?
How many embryos do you foresee?

How long will it take for you
to make a significant contribution?
What can you do for us other candidates can't?

Have you ever been arrested, convicted of
theft, recalcitrance, reckless eyeballing?
Past problems following directives?
Have you signed with SNAP?

What kind of car do you drive?
Will you hold me when I cry?

Neil Silberblatt

Notes on an Unveiling

When she was asked at that terminus
"Do you know the date," she could not
explain how our lunar calendar
differs from their Roman version.

How we do not venerate, or care for,
two-faced Roman gods, like Janus,
or emperors, like Julius or Augustus,
bequeathing their names to months.

She could not explain
how our months celebrate seasons
of planting and harvest, or the raining of
manna, or the building of shelters.
How we do not celebrate the new month
by ripping pages from a calendar
but by prayers welcoming the new full moon
as we welcome the Sabbath bride.

How our new year is marked, not by
champagne or feasting, but by
reflections and fasting for the
pain we have caused.

How Jewish boys are cut
8 days after birth—
one day after He had rested from
the exhausting work of creation.
Or how the arrival of Jewish girls
is a secret known only to their exhausted mothers.

The clerk who posed the question,
and who conferred on her a new birth
of the new year, would have made
no sense of these answers.

He might have marked her
undesirable or returned her to her mother
country, where her story would have ended

in an unmarked ditch near Kiev,
rather than in this sweet earth near Belmont Racetrack.

So, as she approaches that terminus,
we will etch that fictitious date
in granite above the words
"Beloved Wife, Mother and Grandmother,"
and celebrate—at long last—
her many seasons of planting and harvest
as we would bid farewell
to the Sabbath Queen.

Vicki Iorio

My Magical Mothers

Joan of Arc, Joan of Rivers, Jane of Calamities, Helen-of-the-bra-company-Troy, Joy-of-mops-Mangano, Helena-of-make-women-beautiful-Rubenstein, Estee-of-ecstasy-Lauder. My mother never

persevered, manicured, pedicured, never cured me. She never told me where we came from. There is a whispering of Spain, Holland, Lithuania. Picture a film noir map—fast moving arrows always one step ahead of Jew-haters.

Cousin Anna, a giant of a woman, chanteuse from Russia, left me ruby earrings too heavy for my lobes. She is buried in Brooklyn somewhere near Houdini and is missed by her transvestite landlord and her circus friends. This, my mother does not tell me.

I find a sepia tint of Great Aunt Mary, rumored to have traded her infant
daughter for a visa. My mother turns her back on history when I ask for information. She tells me I came out of American air with no claws to the past.

She does talk about the women on my father's side, the barrel-figured ones I resemble. Peasants who remind her of donkeys.

Kyle Potvin

Like a wasp in the wall

Go small.

Shed the fur of your home
and the lawn of gnawed bones.

Don't whimper as your fingers loosen
on Lessing and Murdoch and Kenyon.

Go small
a drip down the drain.

No mercy on what once
promised something.

You are light, unencumbered
as the crystal glass you now fill.

Your mother and grandmother drank from it, too,
with roses, buds and blooms, acid-etched.

With your fingertip, trace its story.
Hear its bell-like toll. Now sip.

Janet Barry

Campfire, with Memories and Music

I know when darkness comes knocking   please forgive the cliché   but it is true, darkness
sniffs around and finds what looks like a cozy nest   some quilts rotting away that grandma
made   some pine boughs snapping in a winter cold that took my breath away   I know the
way to cozy up   the flames reach sap and flare   for just a moment   warmth wedded to
hissing venom   one day I declared it was all okay   I decided   there was no enemy   no
horror in the flame no fear in the darkness   the next day there was sunshine   and a duck
swimming and content on the pond   please forgive   the duck consumed bread that will kill
her and the flames consume wood long dead and well seasoned   I know when cycles come
knocking   bothering me with their tedious predictability   grandma sewed a heart into
one
of her quilts gave it to me as I struggled with cancer   the predictable personal disaster   it's
just that I love the duck   and I want to throw bread at it and watch its iridescent neck reach
for food and be glad about it   it's just that I also love the darkness want to sing low pitched
chants as it snuffles around the firelight to find a place just outside the realm of spark and dy
ing hiss Hey Jude we bed down with only what we can imagine   Hey Jude we wake with
what?   A dose of terror and a bit of hope?   Cotton coddled in desperate prayerful stiches
there is a red heart stitched into the quilt   it beats when I swaddle the cliché   it smells of
stale cigarette smoke   I hear the fire dying   I fall asleep waiting for the loon to sing   the
darkness to pull back   I know I have already heard   enough.

Xiaoly Li

Fox Kits

Four kits run around
through thorny roses,
one with a big black rat
dangling in his mouth.

On a rocky hill
their mother watches,
curling up her fluffy tail
around her nose.

You had not called me Mother yet
when I left you for my first flight,
chasing a dream more than
six thousand miles away.

You followed your friend,
called her mother, "Mom."

These kits will depart
to start their own lives
when leaves begin to fall.

How or can they survive now
if their mother is not here?

I wasn't there to see
your first steps' magic.

I missed your innocence
and your smiles that
melted everyone's hearts.

It was your grandma
who carried you dancing for hours
when you cried in the night.

It was your grandpa
who chewed fresh fish first
then fed them to you.

I walk toward the kits and
they immerse in their game.

Boughs of the weeping cherry tree
sway in the breeze near the den,
their flowers fly like snow and
I start to cry, hard.

Lynn Patmalnee

Leaving the Motherland

I pledged allegiance to the dream
we would find asylum at sea,
but there were only jellyfish
tentacles, tangles, venom
of forgetting, sting of assimilation.

A blind man bound to his wheelchair
sobs at a stained table, calls out
to his wife in the old country,
begging her to dance.

I brush beard hairs and cookie crumbs
from my mother's empty lap,
sand from the shores
of the new world.

Sherine Gilmour

Tired Parent Wanting Poem

I want to be in a hot tub filled with macaroni and cheese.

I want to be sleeping alone in a large bed.

I want to be surfing the Internet for new shoes, too expensive for our budget.

I want to be asleep while having sex and eating mac-n-cheese.

I want to sleep-sex with someone famous and beautiful, but I can't think
of anybody right now.

I want to stop hearing bad news.

I want the Internet to be only pictures of kittens or babies, not quick news bytes about
children killed by shooters, children raped by officers, suicide, global warming, polar ice caps.

I want a day when all I have to do is look at other people's tattoos and laugh.

I want to be cryogenically frozen with my family, then wake to find the economy is better,
my son's health problems have been solved, and I've won the lottery. And trees everywhere
blooming pink buds.

I want the world to sink outside my door, so I can look out at a gulf of blue.

I want to survive, bones quaking radioactive blue cracks. Rattling still with thunder, my feet
firmly planted, the meter inside me ticking down from 50,000 BTUs to 5,000 btus to 1 to 0.

I want to unlock the clanking metal door, slide the rusty bar, open to a world scraped,
flung, made new. To my son, "Here's our world. Let's go look for bluebirds, let's go look for
cardinals."

Caitlin Grace McDonnell

Measure of Grace

The longest person's eyelashes were ten inches,
or maybe six. I think 8. She lived in China,
my daughter tells me, who is nine, like the
youngest soccer coach, in Barcelona, which,
she says, is the best. The length of your integrity
is directly correlated to your forearm in prayer.
If you want to be seen as a woman, wear a string
of pearls. If you want to be seen as everything,
make yourself scarce. Math is comforting, my
daughter says, because the answers are clear.
Meanwhile, the length of time between school
shootings decreases at a rate comparable
to the disappearance of the words "climate change"
from government documents. Or the disappearance
of ice in the Arctic sea, or honeybees from warm
habitats. Yesterday, Sudan, the last Northern White
Rhino was put down in Kenya. The buds that bloom
beneath my daughter's breasts are harder than
I remember on my own body, my own breasts,
whose alveoli no longer make milk. If you squint
at two women, they can almost be one.

Ann E. Wallace

Closed

Close the door.
She looks at me like I am ridiculous.
But I only left it open for a minute.

A girl raised by a father has not
had to think much about the reasons
a family of girls keeps the door closed
and locked.

A family of girls knows
the unwanted will enter
closed doors, will penetrate locks
uninvited.

We do not need to leave
the door open for them.

Hali Sofala-Jones

An Explanation to You Who Will Never Be Born I

Because I was born of two worlds colliding.
My dad smelling still of taro root hot from the fire pits
and my mother white as a thin slip of snow
dusting the Ohio hills of her childhood home.
Because I am a half-bodied thing with a broad nose
and a broad back and a body that calls for some heavy load
to carry from boundary line to boundary line.
Because my tongue is forked, shiv-sliced down the middle,
not a clean break. Because when I sit on the stones in Samoa,
the full-blooded, call me palagi, afakasi. Because I am half-bred,
half-breed: not a pure thing. Because over the years I've chased
each race, embraced my place as *other* no matter what lines
of ancestry I trace. Because there are days when I want to blame
my parents for not thinking of what this half-caste skin would do to me,
what a tight rope walker I would have to be.

An Explanation to You Who Will Never Be Born II

If you were born,
we would always be strangers,
your skin more milk than honey
because he, your father, my love, is palagi.
My heart has room and my body
would gladly spread fat for you,
but child, you would be the birth of fears
for me. Your face only an echo
of what I claim to be.
And who would teach you
to walk each day in your skin?
How could I look into your eyes
and not mourn the loss of Samoan?

Juanita Kirton

Rage

My feets was made to hold this earth
long and wide
Stood firm, clenched up my
big boy bulging inside
he don come when the first leaf fell
Autumn, good as any time to land
planted my toes deep in the soil
he slid out
on a warm bed of fresh fallen mound
a whimper slipped from his smooth pink lips

It was then I lost my mind
bled out fractured blood
his skin black as midnight
I could not protect him
the whip of injustice
seared itself against the membrane
the peel of laughter replaced cries for freedom
No Peace
righteousness mowed down
shot in the back
bolted rage emptied my body
swallowed in salty tears
no heaven can hold this river of pain

There is space at the root where forgiveness lies
in my hell there are gates
and I pray
knees bent
hands on the trigger

Alison Stone

Filling the Eggs

Though it's the hunt that delights them,
I place stickers, candy, glitter hair ties
in the plastic shells.
An even number, labeled
with their initials to prevent arguing.

My lastborn wants a younger sibling.
Otherwise I'll never have
someone to boss around. She doesn't understand
how a woman's body winds down,
or hear, when I stand up, my joints
make noises like a closing door.

I watch from the porch as my daughters
forage through the flowerbeds in filmy
dresses, a tumult of blossoms
beneath their eager hands.
Their baskets loaded with eggs.

Dayna Patterson

Multipara

parous my body pair us spare us
postpartum tedium pair us once

more your parousia on a scale from
apocalypse to epiphany

the fairest I'd cherish my body
multiparous placenta once more

porous sieving my body's blood to
your ferrous forming, bloodborn blooming

parous my body multichorus
once more double heartbeat spare us the

empty nesting restless guessing the
moonswipe left for yes and clean cotton

no blood blooms on shower floor pair us
once more in womb's sacristy red rooms

your parousia at the cusp of my
failing fertility's door once more

parous pair us before oocytes
I've stored from birth pop pomegranate

seeds from ovary's pith and thousands
reabsorbed in flesh or flushed I miss

the feel of fetus quickening feet
knocking rib door not nulliparous

not primiparous I'd relish your
advent viviparous my body

your body adore nesting doll in
marian blue idol in crimson

shrine homunculus my body's years
pare down to whittle and shroud so crown

me little savior little *savoir*
I'd savor life once more parous pair

us pear my body to autumnal
swell I'd call mine I'm calling encore

Lauren Banks

After That Week

The tomato plants were still alive.
Their arms had turned to pale green
some of the leaves were sun-crisp.

I picked three ripe red, almost-split ones and
a bowl full of orange cherry tomatoes.

There was this
and the cab driver who didn't understand
that I could have a wife
who I explained baptism to—
the baby, water, and promises.

He told me about the golden spoon of honey
the Imam whispering in the baby's ear—
our religions, the same, he said.

One true God.
Things begotten, not made.

Lauren Banks

Mother Line

My grandmother and mother birthed
their daughters at 15 and 20.
They used their broad shoulders and muscular legs
and their good, heavy breasts.

I press the small pill through the foil-backed pack
to sync my body with my wife's body
because the crash of her waves against my waves
cannot make a child.

But if it's a daughter
whom I one day carry,
the pearl of my wife inside the oyster of my body,
will she swim like I swim?

Her shoulders swanning through the waves.

Tina Kelley

For My Birth Mother on the Night She Learned I was Reaching Out to Her

My son has asked, do butterflies miss
their mother? Is there a mommy longlegs?

We are under the same northeastern stars.
Will anything happen? Will it be good?

And I think of the possible traits
of all my unknown blood relatives.

Is it from you and yours that I get
my deep love of wide open spaces

like downs, The Palouse, our yard,
Prospect Park and Ellensburg?

Is my fear of hand injuries yours,
and that pleasure from picking a ready scab?

Are you behind the words I can never spell,
mosquitoes, graffiti, harassment, tomatoes?

What are the things I don't know about myself
that I would learn only through resemblance?

You have never loomed large, brave lady.
I don't think there's enough credence given

to adoptees who aren't
ruined by adoption.

But I need, from you, medical history.
I am the most afraid I've ever been.

I want, for you, the chance to say thank you,
And not to worry, I turned out ok.

Callista Buchen

Release

I initial *here and here*, endorse the consent so I can get back to my body, as if the son cares about letters, as if paperwork can contain this wave. My body has its own permission. The nurse wants me to lie down.

I have been fully informed, the forms say. Indeed, this time, I kneel on the bed, face the wall. I growl and bear, my body yawning as the son slips out, the nurses surprised, the closest doctor pulled from the hallway arms out and still shouting, *Do you intend to give birth in this position? Do you intend to give birth in this position?*

This time, I look at the placenta, I look at the stained sheets, this time I look at the baby. Even when I roll over, pull him to my chest, I am on my knees, always, these days, on my knees, the son and I signed in blood. *I have read and understand.* I cut the cord myself.

Milk Drunk

I am pearl and shine, mirror and magic, a vine that rivers across bodies. Swim, swim, it whispers. I build and dissolve, droplets as bricks, cement as evaporation. I am light rain, hard rain, thunder, hail. What leaves a mark and crinkles underfoot.

We are lashed with milk. Versions float, creamed and sticky, a dilated eye. I am rope and tether and you are the kick, kick, the reach and pull *(swim away, swim away)*. We could drown in what drips down my belly, in your arch and cough. You lap. I am a lake, the heat that comes, what absorbs. I turn, I spoil, I empty and dry, even forget.

Rosemary Royston

What the Granny Woman Knows

— *With anything that's born th' mothers have t'suffer.*
Mrs. Echols, *Foxfire 2*

Even so, to cut a hemorrhage
slide an axe, blade side up,
under the bed. For fever,
a bowl of water.

A sharp knife under the pillow
is rumored to slice pain down
to tolerable bits. To ease delivery,
sip nettle. To bring on labor, rue.

Carrying bloodstone in the left pocket
wards off miscarriage, just as
having your partner draw a talisman
on your belly during a new moon.

Never, ever, spin wool, knit,
or leave anything with a knot
in the house of the mother,
or the umbilical cord may strangle.

Babies born with a caul are gifted.
Dry and preserve the caul, keep pieces
in a locket or small bag for protection,
mix with herbs for a healing potion.

Julia C. Alter

Ode to My Kumquat (10 Weeks)

Today you are bizarre and foreign,
un-reachable black sand beach.
Fingernails and peach fuzz. I hear
the hooves of your heartbeat
through the Doppler, sure stampede
that crushes and creates me in an instant,
releasing bright, bitter mist. I don't know
what to tell you. Everyone wants
to coat you in sugar, turn you into
dessert. I close my eyes and bite
through fluorescent skin. My ducts
water, lips pucker. So much stranger
than I could have imagined. You keep me
up at night like too many sweets
or cheap liquor. But you pull me
from sleep with your purity,
your crispness. You are citrine,
crystalline. In spite of the mud
inside, you emerge, you clarify.

Jen Stewart Fueston

Night Shift

Night is a mouth,
hungry and endless
in its demands.

You offer your body,
its brief power
to soothe and quiet.

Sometimes you're enough.
Through sleeplessness
you tell yourself

this is the easy part.
Be grateful for the pangs
that are quieted by milk,

the hungers that respond
to flesh. Holding him
you know there will be nights,

like yours, when nothing will
satisfy, that an open mouth
can wait forever to be filled.

Robbie Gamble

Lippes Loops

Babysitters tucked us in often, my parents
away at conferences, or hosting
dinners parties: parades of men in tweeds
and women who wrapped themselves
in shiny silk sarongs from missions abroad.
We three brothers listened, and strange
serious words floated up through the bannisters
into our bedroom: *Zero Population Growth*
and *pregnancy rates* and *clinical field trials*
and, of course, *The Great Cause.*
This is how we learned that a man
puts his penis in the woman's vagina,
and then a baby grows in her uterus,
which was a big problem, unless
of course, the baby was planned.
We had been planned, so we knew we were ok.
One night, I remember Mummy dressing
for a big dinner, wearing earrings that twisted
below her hairdo like white plastic snakes.
She called them Lippes Loops,
an important new thing called an IUD.
She blushed when she showed them to us,
like she'd done something a bit naughty,
wearing too much eye makeup,
or leaving her blouse undone
one button too low. They said IUDs worked
by filling up the space inside
the woman's uterus, making it have
a *local foreign body reaction,*
so a baby wouldn't start to grow there.
Grampa found a plastics factory in Hong Kong
that would produce his own loops,
for three cents per unit, before the device
got patented and *the regulators got involved.*
He was going to ship them all over the world,
to Korea, Chile, West Africa, wherever
he thought there might be a problem
with unplanned babies. Grampa hated red tape,

which was what *bureaucrats* tangled him up in
when they wanted to waste his valuable time.
I remember Mummy only wore
those snakey earrings just that once.

Rachel Barton

A Far Cry

He takes his jacket and camera and his designer beverage.
He is going up on the roof. No, he will not come down.
It's not the top of the world but you can see it from here.
After drinking so much Turkish coffee, a thief might enter
Al Jebal's Bazaar wearing his balaclava. This is a college town,
after all, where you can try anything once. He might steal
the plastic crate on the counter full of baklava or the goat
in the freezer. Nothing is flying in the air like lovers and
a violin, not even a rooster, but something is in the air. I
dream of the kid's closet. It is only a niche in the wall with
shelves narrower than a sock. His grey clothes are stuffed
onto the ledges haphazardly. He is not yet established.

He climbs to the roof, dull thuds to my pen's scratches,
then silence. I suppose we all want to climb or fly to a high
place sometimes, up the mountain to an untouched
dome of sky. From there I can see the glacier's runoff—a
braided river frozen in swirls and humps as if only yesterday
or a moment ago it ploughed pell-mell across the valley. I carry
my high place within but he is still young and searching. Cows
calve and so do icebergs but in the valley of now we're talking
orchards or the Old Growth Trail up Vineyard Mountain. This is
a far cry from Turnagain Arm, where Dall sheep and their kids
climb the cliffs on narrow rock ledges, and sheep gazers crane
necks to spot the curved tusks, the scampering white coats.

Jody Burke-Kaiser

The Alchemist, age 3

The alchemist, hopeless,
collects rocks that are shiny,
pockets feathers
as they fall, few and red,
knows the loss of water
poured hand to hand,
has waited all day outside
the barber shop for cut curls.
Rock salt is a gem long
undervalued, the solid part
of the sea. All bright things
must be touched, carried home,
washed with soap.

The alchemist sees eggs,
solid-liquid-solid
are a clue overlooked.
He cannot eat them
without witnessing the pour
from shell to pan.
The best parts of things
are thrown away, live stones
at the center of peaches,
the threads pulled fine
and wet from beans.

Mary Bonina

Mothers Wait

the ferry sank
the ferry jammed
with teenagers

texting for help
that did not come
three hundred
sons and daughters
went under

drowned

on shore
the mothers waited

were waiting
for them
to be rescued

they stayed while
it rained through
the whole rescue
operation that
became a recovery

one mother said
*It's raining
and my daughter
is underwater*

my son is there
in the same country
I think of him always

he takes ferries
out to islands or small
aircraft to other places

Rebecca Hart Olander

Inheritance

It's like I've passed on some ancient true thing
the summer my son drinks a vanilla egg cream
like I do, side by side on swivel stools
in an old-fashioned Nantucket soda shop,
back home, mixes malted Ovaltine into his morning
milk. It's not witchcraft, or rocket science,
but it resonates, makes me feel a little something
of me will travel with him as he moves on.
He's writing graduation thank-you notes, trying
to figure out how to address the women over the fence,
the unmarried Marie and her mother Doris,
who signed their card "Your Proud Neighbors."
He cares about this, and I picture a chamber inside
him, stocked with familiar honey, know
he won't forget where he came from.

Pramila Venkateswaran

Diary Entry, 1930

Yesterday something strange happened. Ambi was running in the yard holding an imaginary rifle, screaming *Doo-doo-thuppakki, police-kaaran pondaati.* It is funny, but how does he know what a rifle looks like, what it does, how it sounds, how to hold it? He's never seen one. Unless he has been looking at the newspapers his father reads and has seen pictures of British soldiers with guns. I know war is on in Europe and the East Indies—radio broadcasts, news reels before movies at the local Lotus Cinema we have been to a couple of times with Ambi are filled with the smells and sounds of war—but Ambi's world is just school and cricket and pranks. Our police only carry sticks, not guns, and they are hardly seen in our neighborhood except when they come during Diwali for gifts. A sad lot, most of them, really, and their pay is so bad, they look hungry, barely able to defend themselves, let alone us. That stupid rhyme, I know, it's nonsense, lots of kids sing it, but it makes me shiver. I tried pulling that imaginary rifle from him and he chased me with it screaming that rhyme: *I am the innocent wife shot by my policeman husband.*

Sara Moore Wagner

What He Tears Down Cannot be Rebuilt
— *after Job*

A gust cyclones the grass clippings
up from the driveway, past
my mother who sits in the sun
with a red face like an open flower.
I think maybe a hand, God's hand, is in that whirl
of foliage which comes to rest near my son
who jumps over and over into
his tiny plastic pool until all the water
is gone. I don't tell him *stop now.* I don't
know why—it's pretty dangerous,
that smack of skin on dry plastic—
over and over. In this moment, though,
with the sun holding its own
great hot palm over my mother, that beautiful
boy, over me, over the red-winged blackbird
who scolds my own little baby every time he leaves
his leaping to part a curious branch,
pudgy fingered and wide eyed— we are ok.
Here is my mother and here am I. Here he is.
Here is a glass of water and a carton
of blackberries. Take as much as you want.
Move on.

Renuka Raghavan

Good Ones

She's wearing a pink chiffon hijab,
picking out a watermelon and
talking to someone via Bluetooth.
A tiny cherub face peaks at me from
around his mother's waist.
I wave and whisper, *Hello*.
He grins, timid and unsure.
He temporarily disappears
back into his mother's gauzy folds.

She moves on to the cantaloupes,
as I pick up a watermelon and tap on it
with my ear against the hard rind,
just like my mother taught me.

An old man pushes his cart up to me and says,
Looks like you know how to pick out the good ones.

The little boy steps out again,
this time openly laughing at my
watermelon choosing process. So
I laugh too. He points his fingers,
thumb in the air, index finger extended toward me.
Pew, pew, pew, soft boyish
sounds imitate. I drop my watermelon into
the cart with exaggeration,
feigning a wounded hit.
He laughs, triumphant.

The old man says,
They really start training them young, don't they?
He'll get big and blow shit up for Allah like they do.
I wouldn't encourage him, if I were you.
The mother hears and smacks her son,
admonishing his behavior.
The cherub weeps as he's dragged out of the store
by his angered, humiliated mother.
Their cart with a watermelon and two cantaloupes, left unattended.

It's too bad you can't spot the good ones,
I want to say to the old man,
but he's moved on.

I watch as he digs through a pile of greens to find
the best-looking spinach.

Kristy Webster

Sons

One of you has taken more after your father. DNA and Cola, his nature versus my nurture.

My father dies.

My sons bring me girls. I offer them bowls of popcorn, but they don't stay long. I've never been one of those girls, carefree giggles and no plans. I spit old-girl chips on their cupcakes. Watch out, that bit of frosting on your nose. There. No, there.

Tea pots. Never owned one.
I carved coffee holes. I bleed Folgers.

In my forties I'll dry out. The desert. Ceramic bowls. I'll burn, never having burned like this before.

Sons. Babies. My sons and their igloos. My sons and my age. My love.
They'll lie to me. Tell me I was a saint.

I'll pity their lover-girls. Thinking: babies, more sons, age, delivery and doubt.
Don't forget weekends, weeks and ends, and matricide.

My books. My crippled dog will eat them.

The moon gives me cramps. The sun brings me pebbles. Grains. Mortuaries. I am spent grief.

Fathers are what you bump into. Fathers are missions.

I am forty-one. You two with your cars, your places with girls and beanstalks. You've brought me four.

In my dreams, I am eleven, dark, lanky, suitable for play dates and teasing playground princesses with earthworms.

Awake, I am Elijah. Sitting.

I am fifty-two and have taken to pottery. For birthdays I still hand you the moon.

Crystal Karlberg

Watching a Video of Owls Flying in Slow Motion Makes Me Think of You

Losing you is like feathers,
the most beautiful ones.

I once found the feather of a blue jay
but I left it behind because they're so mean.

I held it for a long time though
and turned it towards the sun.

My throat is full of seeds
I want to feed you, but you

were born a forager, a quiver
on the air I couldn't hold on to.

The sound of your wings
swallows me. From a distance

fog looks like smoke. You
used to fit into my elbow, a tiny

fire I stoked myself. Now
you're a mist. From

a distance is the only way
I can see you.

Tasslyn Magnusson

When I Say I Mean

When I say I'm an alcoholic,
I mean I haven't had a drink in eighteen years.

When I say I haven't had a drink in eighteen years,
I mean any alcohol at all whatsoever.

When I say any alcohol at all whatsoever,
I mean even though alcohol whispers to me.

When I say alcohol whispers to me,
I mean the time I was in South Africa by myself.

When I say the time I was in South Africa by myself,
I mean right after my son was born.

When I say right after my son was born,
I mean when I planned how I could hurt him.

When I say I planned how I could hurt him,
I mean I worried I wanted to suffocate him.

When I say I worried I wanted to suffocate him,
I mean it was non-stop.

When I say non-stop,
I mean I bit my hand because I thought it was going to hurt him.

When I say I bit my hand because I thought I was going to hurt him,
I mean I had to do it a lot because the hand wouldn't stop.

When I say a lot,
I mean look at my moon mother scars eclipsing my freckles.

When I say look at my moon mother scars eclipsing my freckles,
I mean look at the miracle we survived.

Allison Adair

Raising a Girl, 2018

My palm on her forehead is the new reflex.

In the blue night hours, terrifying dreams

mash together with the room's true sounds:

cat claw plucking a drawer's joint. Horsehair

stirring, as an insect lifts its leg. Downstairs

on the street, a man punches the air. Fear

blazes up into a sun, to feed raw sense.

I stand there. Watch her breathe.

Teri Cross Davis

Co-sleeping

Years later when they are teenagers, out studying
the art of lying and partying, I am told I will
treasure this shallow sleep, two- and four-
year-old feet in my back and stomach, soft
bodies fattened by my milk, such slight impressions
they make on a queen-sized mattress. My weight, a well,
sinks them closer. I breathe in the stupor of their sweet-rot
scent—*my children*. I loll the words in my mouth like a chewed
pacifier. Listen to each tiny chest expanding and contracting,
secure and within reach. *My children*—I swaddle the fact of them.
Fold the blood-borne knowledge tight, tuck in its edges, wrap it again.
On this night—their bodies burrowed in tangled sheets, parental bed
both temple and fortress, their vitality is nearness and sacrosanct, yet look—
already, they grow— leaving me in a moment perfect only in memory.

Kathleen Mitchell-Askar

Kingdom of Lost Teeth

Like a groundhog your shadow means long childhood
and I play fairy to your penciled questions
about a realm I've invented loss by loss

I'm tired of this and I've no place
else to put your tooth but in my soft robe
I'm the last place you would look

By morning three coins bloom silver in your palm
and its snowing again all white pulp and bicuspid cold
you've made me swear
on our only visible bones
that there is this someplace else

Judy Swann

Just the High Lights

My name is Mom, unless there is an emergency
and then my name is Mom Mom Mom.
Nobody wants the fully-narrated, 3-hour life,
just me at the sink, eating tuna out of the can.

And so my name is Mom Mom Mom
and as it was in Middle English, I embody sadness as a skill
just me at the sink, eating tuna out of the can
because a very little bit of the world suffices.

As was understood in Middle English, I see sadness as a skill,
a concept meaning something like 'wisdom' or 'kindness'
but a very little bit of the real-world suffices
to unmask me as a poser, make me giggle in my mugshot.

And as I make a dash for 'wisdom' and 'kindness'
my name is Mom, unless there is an emergency
and then I am unmasked as a poser, giggling in my mugshot.
Nobody wants the fully-narrated, 3-hour life.

Cammy Thomas

Puzzle

I wash plates and cutlery, and shape
my papers into graceful piles.

I put the kids to bed in their flimsy forts,
reading them the same books over and over.

I tend my little dog, and lay out
a thousand-piece puzzle

of a painting by Canaletto,
tiny Venice under robin's egg blue.

Every day, we put a couple of pieces in,
until even the difficult sky begins to take shape.

Screech owls whinny in our woods at night,
and the highway sighs in the distance.

In the morning, I cut heavy white peonies
beaded with water, falling apart

as I touch them, pinch bugs dropping
and running on the kitchen table.

Sara Moore Wagner

It Must Be So Exhausting

I am having trouble
deciding on accurate space
between the words and my
split toenail, whether they are
the same, whether I am selfish
for mentioning this jagged
part. If you think I am better
than this, you are right, and also:
you are better—and also
that I will always say I am better
because I am afraid of what
you're looking at. Listen,
I was a spider in a past
life and I learned to speak
my name in webs across
the front of your house, and you
sprayed me with the hose,
and you washed me.
I was your grandmother who
was never naked in front of any
one, even her husband, your
cancer-ridden father.
I will make everything
about myself because I don't
know what space is.
Also, I am a bitch, Also—
there will never
be enough space to stop me
moaning at the foot of your bed.
I was that dog in the picture
you showed our son,
the one whose head eclipsed
the buttons on your mother's dress.
And you wish
you had shot it, and
you wish I would stop talking
about pain. About it. About
myself like this.

Jane Yolen

Scars

I saw my mother undressed once.
There were ribbed scars on her back.
I rubbed my point finger
lightly over one of the ridges.
She shuddered at my touch.
I asked her if it hurt.
She said it was a reminder,
her voice almost cooing.
I was too young to understand.
Years later when they took my wings,
before I could even stretch them,
before the air had foiled around them,
I remembered that day. My daughter
and her daughters will never go
under that particular knife.
I will keep them safe, hidden
till the wind can lift them.
There is so much sky.

Wendy Cannella

Glovebox

What if Robert Frost left me a message
in the glovebox of the rusted car
abandoned on the farm, 1966.

I am clinging to *How to Grow Zinnias.*
A hand extends from the cover of the book,
pulling me into the ground. I play my

broken cello in a mother-language
of brokenness. If I find the note, what if
it says the afterlife is like a riverbed: full, empty.

Kate Hanson Foster

Cockcrow

How soft the early light—like an inner thigh.

And then a patchwork of white warnings—sucking

the night out shade by shade.   This is the moment

my body rejects itself—a mismatch of chemicals

refusing to be corrected. I reach for my mouth

and feel the everything of emptiness.   Light

that tugs on my nerves.   Light that sears and singes

my worth.   I was a wife.   Light that makes the fog

foggier. I was a mother. Outside the pines

are swaying in the morning sun—new ends

growing and reaching to please it.   I had a mind.

I had ideas.   And a beast seeps through unweaving

me thread by thread,   turning its bundle

of claws—   I was I was I was.

Jane Attanucci

Passing My Younger Self on the Beach: A Cento

Birds afloat in air's currents
some children run after each other squealing in the shallows
    near but not too near
she seems to want to be both caught and free
—watching rather   the spaces of sand between them

the sun-warmed sand   the surf   this reunion
a to and a from   and an urgency
her mind full to the wind   I see her plunge
return for a snack of them   with gobbling mother-eye
thinking sweetness sweetness

Sources: Denise Levertov, Marie Howe, Elizabeth Bishop, Anna DiMartino, Gail Mazur, Brenda Shaugnnessy, Adrienne Rich, Gwendolyn Brooks and Sylvia Plath.

Iris Jamahl Dunkle

Acceptance Speech, or How to Be a Martyr

Hello. I join you here today from an outcropping of land. From limestone-bedded soil. From salt on wind. From the over-bloom of too much rain. From trying to stay above that throb of earth.

We are born to it. Two feet on the very ground we will be buried in.

Can you smell it? That rot and beauty?

My mother keeps telling me she is dying. She lives a hundred yards away, but she may as well live in my ear. She buzzes like yellowjackets infesting the whole property. She populates and hides in bare stalks like poison oak in winter. (We are afraid to use Roundup, given the studies).

My mother has been collecting tumors in her belly like eggs. They hide in the tall grass of her abdomen. She says she's keeping them. She says they are hers alone.

Every year at Easter we roll back that big stone and fill the field with bright plastic eggs. Some are never found. Some, we find years later, bloated, rotted.

But, this year, the sky kept opening its jaw until I couldn't bear it anymore. I stood on the porch watching the spectacle. I stood on the porch asking the sky for a god-damned break. But, the sky wouldn't listen. The house closed in. My mother followed me like a comet. My mother orbited me like a giant moon. Leaving a trail not of breadcrumbs but of guilt. Those thick stones I've been swallowing for forty-three years.

Can I say now that I'm sinking?

In closing, I just want to remind you that good daughters don't want their mothers to die.

In closing, I would like to remind you that the deer don't even get up anymore when I startle them while trying to find places to hide the eggs.

In closing, I want to tell you the sky is made of nothing except air and light. Grey as stone. Heavy as all hell.

What did those women think when they walked into that cave and found nothing? No body. Just a message hidden in the wet earth. Pushing up in the buds on the trees. Throbbing. Saying, *You must believe in it to tell it.*

In closing, I want to say, I am not a good daughter. I have not found all the fucking eggs. And I have no desire to look anymore.

Stephanie Angelini

A Mother And Daughter Speak Of The Past

Encapsulated
So you can drink
Down with a glass
Of milk or water
So were my mother's words
Of her own mother
Short where the story was long
One short story
Over and over
Rolled and balled up
Small, but not enough to swallow,
Swallow and keep down

Carla Panciera

To Our Boldest Child

You marched ahead of us
down every trail,
sometimes naked.
Hands behind your back,
you nosed snakes and hornets.

How we dreaded
playground climbing structures,
parking lots,
the stepladders stock boys left
in the Home Depot aisle.

We were unprepared for you,
couldn't anticipate impulse:
tasting battery acid, for example,
or the pink plastic egg
that fit so perfectly in your throat.

You don't climb up *the slide,*
we might have said—
*then tumble back
and have your bone set
without morphine.*

So, we were relieved
when you didn't
like to swim.
Bubble strapped to your back,
you kept dry.

Poolside, we read.
We had almost forgotten
reading. Yes, we thought,
this is what it feels like
to look away.

And that day, we didn't hear
the splash, only
the slap of feet
on concrete, the silence
of you, mid-air.

We sprang up
out of our own shoes as you
exploded to the surface spouting water,
an oracle who foretold:
There is nothing left but fear.

Megan Merchant

Smear

I am told that I was a terrible child, a crimp in her hopes.

A blown glass flower where an orchid should have bloomed
given how much she cared.

My mother swaddled my feet in wet cotton, then covered
them in wool.

She was told if, when I woke, the wraps had dried,
there was a chance I could be saved.

If still wet, I would grow to crave that slick between my legs.

And if, after three days, the egg she slid under my bed
cracked with blood, it meant the malignancy was drained,

and I would go on to be loved by a Saint.

I was told the night she learned I was coming,
she took the brightest paint and blotted a paper with prayers,

then folded it in half, grieved when the colors mucked gray.

Suzanne Edison

Assaying Praise

We sing on Sundays, lift up
eyes and hands beyond this mortal sky,

join voices with the air, pull down
succor from this routine.

At home the window shade flaps
open showing smudges on the pane,

mother upbraids us,
her tongue lashing like switchgrass,

for whatever is unworthy of sunlight—
as if the pulsing, plumbed beneath our skin,

isn't laced with hunger for caress
or sharp with jealousy—as one child appears

to receive the drug of favor over
another. Sieved and parsed is praise—

yet prized—and like the swelling beet
whose harbored liquor is sluiced sweet

within its meat, we wait for its release.
Wait, while a storm-brewed beating

pounds its leafy tops; wait for those green
flags to rebound. Then, we sing about

what, each day, can't be lowered.

Sharon Tracey

Solo Hike on the Wilderness Coastal Trail
—*Olympic National Park, Washington*

I walk beside the slosh-talking,
that median strip of sea-beach—
listening to surf-speech
stepping over long bones

of driftwood, clumps of kelp
hanging their copper hair
on blue rocks. The birds
are black turnstones.

I've crossed wet headlands—
slipped on too many banana slugs.
I've washed my long hair
with a gallon of spring water,

a daughter who has read both
Bible and tide charts, who
thinks she saw the face of God
in the Pacific near Cape Alava.

I reach the petroglyphs at low tide—
whale and hunter-faces carved
long ago by the Makah tribe. With
a stone, bone, or wooden maul,

it's hard to tell. This place is called
Wedding Rocks. Why I don't know—
I see so many walking here alone.
My mother said: *Go, don't call me.*

Carol Dorf

Mother, Can You Explain Again?

Maman, my spider, contains the house
beneath her long jointed legs.

Why is the desire for more cake suspect
while the desire for more sex admirable?

Those bulbs. It never was about lighting —
I wish I could say it was about the rule book

but she was overwhelmed with her own
anxieties or sacked out on the sofa.

She was the kind who worried her food.
Now she's stopped talking, prelapsarian.

Anne Pluto

Triolet

Your daughter never will give you quiet
the past, a house of splinters, wedges inside her heart
and she will keep it there pulsating and tight.
Your daughter will never give you quiet
she will not hear your story despite
what you have kept hidden tears you both apart.
Your daughter will never give you quiet
instead, she'll call, and fall, a fat and broken sweetheart.

Carol Barrett

Entry

Late day I return
to Coyote Mesa. Two
lizards scramble

either side
of the door, this
temporary stucco

home, their long
stripes curved
like boomerangs,

spots on their backs,
dozens of eyes.
They cling to the wall

while I enter, then
scurry to another
station. Inside,

my daughter
has left me
supper—broccoli

flowerets, a small
bowl of hummus,
pistachios.

Here are wash basin,
journal, lamp
for when the day

moves on
like the small
creatures

sharing this haven.
I need
for nothing.

Megan Merchant

I work the tangled

clumps free with a comb, pinching
the root to deaden the pull.

My mother's hair is a nest for memories
that sloughed in the night.

Feather vain & gale. I spray the knot
with olive oil & taste the lake

we floated in when I was a child.
Summer muck that felt smooth

to the bottoms of my feet when
I grazed the floor swimming, until

I stood to wave & it sucked me down,
bed of algae, mayflies, & leaves—all dying.

When I cannot free her strands into silk,
I take the scissors & try to cut along the shoreline.

Kathleen Mitchell-Askar

Profile

How far I can listen, daughter
I knew you had a cigarette
and that the bus exhaled you
by its airy outrush

seated on the blue stained bench
chipped off
your face in profile
with one eye
a facet faced away
where you need me like an appendix
vestigial

some swelling *-osis* of hearing
by *-itis* calved from me
like iceberg or whale
at the thinnest edge of listening
I blur

beyond that
your ear takes over for my ear
and here I
am cochlear and inept

Lavinia Kumar

Not a Variable

My mother, a constant
not *a, b,* or *c,* just *m*

predictable, as with buoyancy,
gravity, a number,

a number used in differentiation,
integration—our letters across water,

the pen and paper glue, our ebb, and flow,
tides always guided by a moon,

she in England, we in Ireland
she at work, we in boarding school

held in her butterfly net
and even when we grew

she pulled us in if needed,
whooshed us off when right.

Alexis Rhone Fancher

Residuals: An Elegy

You are a channel-
surfer between here and eternity.

You are canned laughter—
talisman against dead air.

You shield me like white noise.
You are pilot. And then disappear.

Even now, I watch for you,
find you in infomercials

and serial dramas where you are always
an episode ahead of me.

You are the choke in my reality show,
a rerun of tears.

You, sweet boy, are the cancelled series;
you are the remote.

Last night: the same commercial—
a boy's first haircut,

soft curls
sheared, floating.

He could have been your understudy.

Catherine Anderson

Inquiry After the First Anniversary

Is it a plover or a gull?
It is the dog chasing them both.

Does it crash down or gently land?
It seeps up from solid ground.

Do you record it with ink or a screen?
With a knife on the wall.

Does it wake you or put you down?
It wakes me and won't put me down.

Is it black and white or color?
The phone went dead.

Will it come to scraps of bread or meat?
It does not eat.

Is it with you for good?
She is not with me, she is me.

Did you name her before or after?
She is the million names for lost daughter.

Jennifer Jackson Berry

Leather Birthday
— August 6, 2016

Our baby is watermarked, taken outside too soon,
before we had the chance to mildly soap, pat dry—

our baby hangs on my left shoulder.
I reach inside

and do not find umbrellas or ponchos tightly folded.

We are empty and loose—a mother, a father—no,
a woman, a man—we are wet, stinking

of our baby never born.

MaryAnn L. Miller

There is No Word

A woman who has lost
a husband is a widow.
A laid-off woman is
jobless. She lost her job
as if she had
been careless, losing a glove
as she dug for change
at the market.

There is no word
in English for a bereft
mother whose child died.
Such words exist
in other languages: *shakul,*
thakla,
verwaistemutter,
tethligon.
Childless is not for the

woman who did have one
and now doesn't—
this ex-mother,
a semantic lacuna
surrounded by imago,
has been unlatched,
unchilded. A lone word
a syllabic vacuum

is insufficient to her
state. She requires etymology
from an ancient language;
vilomah—
against the natural
order, or a hyphenated word:
grief-eater, hair-puller
dirt-scraper— inside-out-belly.

Lisa DeSiro

Almost ten years later, I dream of a sighting

My father's come to visit, bringing two of my mother's purses. He thinks their long straps are impractical. While discussing the concept of cross-body bags we see a woman walk by the cafe window and, in profile, she looks exactly like my mother. My stomach jolts, my father's face is shocked, we double-take—but then the woman's passed, her back is to us.

Carla Panciera

To the Specialist

You take the same exit, my sister said,
that we used to take for Rocky Hill Fair.

We have few landmarks from our new lives.
Instead, we know the strip mall
where the man lived who made rope halters;
the town where we brought plow blades
to be sharpened; the street in Johnston
where we took calves to be butchered.

Where we baled hay: housing development.
Where we grazed heifers: golf course, parking lot.

The old memories might make me pause—
cattle sudsy with Whisk at the wash racks on show day,
the bloodied snake-pieces in the still-warm bale,
the library-like shelves of tractor parts behind men
who smelled of rubber and diesel.
New rope's splinters in palm flesh, fingers.

Except there's a new thing to consider: The doctor
says something about sugar triggering the dye.

The red areas on the scan show activity.
Activity in my family was, until now,
the most meritable thing. Also a strong back,
the ability to drive standard, a lack of squeamishness.
I don't look away. The lungs. One rib. The spine.
Belatedly, I remember to hold my mother's hand.

The spine, the doctor says, (a bad dresser in a polyester suit,
clogs). *The spine is what worries me most.*

Well, my mother says. A wet day. Another one.
She insists we eat. It's time. So we are in the car
trying to find a breakfast place
on the same road as the Baileys' farm.
The Baileys' farm, at least, still exists.
Everyone dies of something.

They have thick hair, calves, curls
over their polls that you can lock your fingers in.

At the butcher's in Johnston, we woke the calf up,
handed its halter to someone who told us: *Wait here.*
We climbed back into the heated cab, turned the radio up.
Before the song ended, the butcher returned
with the halter, a brown bag filled with tongue and liver
that warmed our laps on the ride home.

Cyn Kitchen

Returning Home After Word that Mom has Died

Praise the rolling Nebraska hills rocking
the window of this long silver train
steeple framed against a high white sky
any given Monday.
Brown pasture scrub-pocked,
fingers of bare tree's arthritic reach
dirt road stretching into nothing
pools of gray March ice's
muted mirror.

Armando blasts from the
intercom—*breakfast is served*
in the dining car
but my appetite like
that mirror
swallows light.

I see a doe
stock still among the trees,
watching us pass
as if in search
of a familiar face.
It's me, I mouth,
fingers to the glass,
but before she sees me
we're gone.

James Hoch

Letter to the Brother

[You Ask What It Was Like]

—she died, I say, like it was
            something she did, like

falling out of bed or a car
            drifting off the road, the woods

eating bright canes of light—
            died like the sound she made,

and the sound the orderlies
            did not, lifting her briefly,

buckle break breath, within—
            you could hear it, we all could,

like trying to move a thing
            heavy or fragile and suddenly

goes sideways, we knew it
            on our faces—a second,

and we were orphaned
            and birthed all over again—

Christine Jones

On You Leaving Home

A monarch pauses

       on a milkweed; I think of you.

At eighteen.   You've realized *chrysalism*

       from the *Dictionary of Obscure Sorrows;*

 also what a mother feels   sending her child

      sweaterless

         through a forest

 of six-needled pine.

***

I believe you when you tell me you're sad,
and when you say you won't wait

until you're dead to be famous.

***

For today, though, I'm content
when you discover the vase

of wild asters painted underneath
Van Gogh's *Three Pairs of Shoes.*

Linda Spolidoro

Facebook

Facebook knows I'm getting old, apparently
thinks I should cover up this summer

insists swim skirts and tankinis
long wavy room-to-breathe tunics
a serum to un-fuck-up my face

I'm only looking out for you, girl
the sensible-shoed fat-thigh reduction creamed
algorithm condescends

I middle-finger an unflattering emoji
right in that shade-throwing bitch's sidebar

Do you kiss your Mother with that mouth? Facebook replies

Because I've noticed your lips are looking a little thin

Lois Roma-Deeley

Riding Past the Cemetery in April

The kids tell me it's bad luck
to breathe in the air of the dead.
But I'm more fearful
of Spring's unpredictable heart—
how the purple mallow and common milkweed
scrambles along the ground,
their roots pushing through and down
rocky soil,
growing and growing,
as if they know where I am going.

Kelly Fordon

Leaving Home
— *After Ghost Town...Memories of Commerce, Texas*
by Jill Slaymaker

Goodbye flatland
goodbye toothless
house   goodbye
catapult of
motherhood
goodbye
dirt-filled mouth
nighttime wine
cookie dough
and crunches
farewell peeling
melamine cabinets
ratty rescue dogs
nearly bald
nearly sexless
nearly dead
goodbye to the bleak
afternoons
above the scrubbed
fields   this
fallow life
sky heathery
the sun slipping
into its raincoat
the wind
a sandwich wrapper
plucked from the trashcan
safe from the
metal grabbers
and those who
thought we were
spellbound.

Jill Slaymaker

75

FICTION

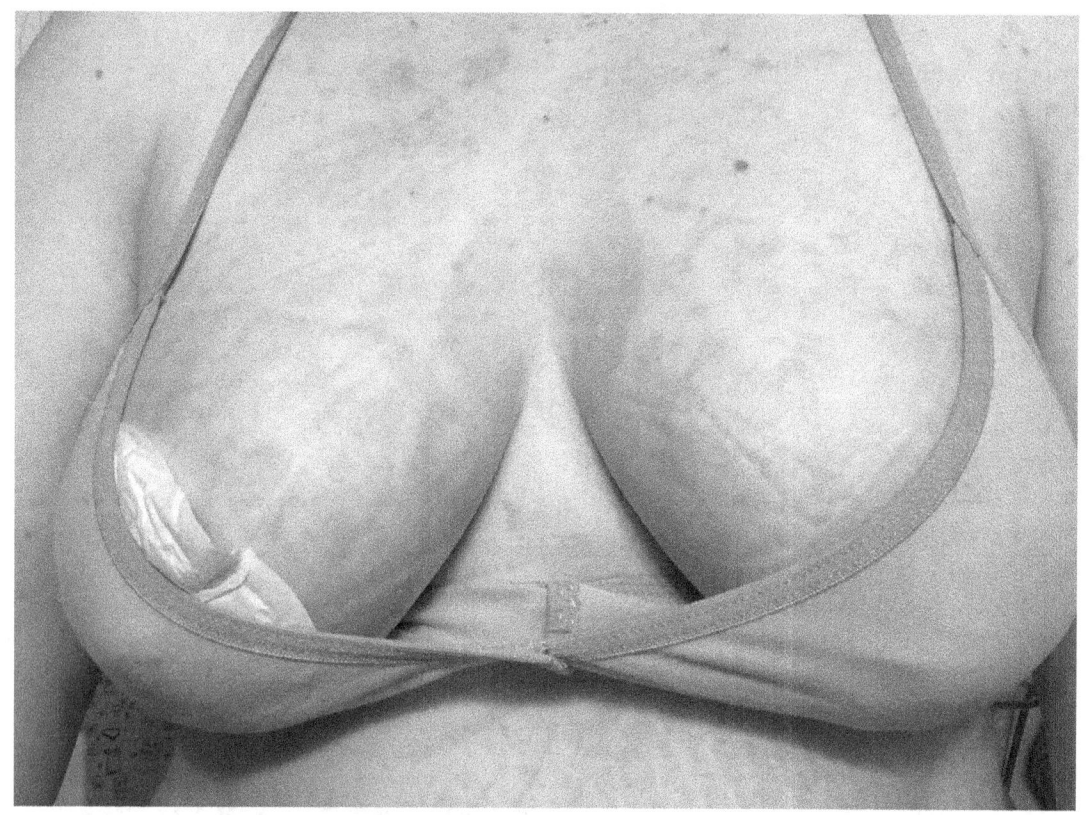

Megan Wynne

Breena Clarke

The Loss of Tilly

My belly swung side to side as I ran from Bledsoe Plantation, still aflame, the scent of burning flesh and fur in the air. I stood on a hillock and watched the house burn, the barn collapse to sticks, the fields become scorched, the harvest lost before the flames were brought to heel.

I ran headlong from that place. I ran until my lungs were fit to bursting. The sky was red and orange and saturated with what had burned off Bledsoe, had traveled with the winds, had settled upon all of the trees and bushes. Saliva dribbled from my mouth. I panted with my head low, my sides heaving and pulsing. I rooted around and found a small stream whose water ran clear. I drank. I looked in the pool into the eyes there and wondered why Tilly had run so far and fast from all that was familiar. I took a whiff of acrid air and recollected. The pigs, the cows, the horses, Him, Her, and All of Them. I smelled all. My distended teats ached with hope and anxiety.

The air was so thick it was a labor to breathe. Coughs tore at my lungs like a ball of meat wrapped around glass shards. My feet burned. I ran when the flames came to eat me. The fire outraced me at first, but I persevered; I out-ran the fire. The stream saved me. Me, my feet and Mine. It restored my healing balm, my saliva and I was able to comfort myself, my feet, and Mine.

Mine were growing. Mine were becoming restless as they must. Mine were coming soon to the world. Mine were already hungry, greedy for any food available. Mine soon to arrive.

I was pulled to a likely whelping place by the comforting aroma of hays and grasses and manures, the smells that reminded me of Bledsoe Plantation before the burning. I scouted a comfortable place in a dark corner of a pleasantly aromatic barn.

Mine squealed to life, one following the next, the next and again and again until all my teats were pulled on by my own Mine in the early hours of a day that came bright and lovely. Oh, Mine! Naked and hungry and rooting against me. I slathered them with balm from my mouth, and I realized a joy that is unmatched.

It came upon us suddenly. It made loud sounds of wonder. It thrust its arms out and advanced upon Mine and me.

"Go! Go! Off with you!"

I could not help but snap Its hand in defense of Mine. I will lay down my life to protect Mine.

"Go! Go! Off with you!" It cried.

I withstood a barrage of rocks from It for as long as I was able. I retreated growling, leaving Mine behind. I heard Mine crying with hunger and smelled It fingering Mine and plucking at their ears. "Mine," I growled low, "are mine alone." I pulled my lips back nearly to my ears.

I returned after dark when It went away. Mine snuggled to me desperately, urgently. They were famished.

At sunrise, It came back. It saw me and gasped. It ran screaming when I snarled. It returned. It thrust a stick at me. "Go! Go!" It barked. I clamped and pulled on the stick. I tried to shake It. It went away and returned pelting me with a barrage of stones one of which landed on my back leg, wounding me. Mine squealed, I howled. It stayed and kept me at bay.

Pain in my injured leg was sharp and constant. I moved very little. Hiding out during the daytime, I dragged myself to be with Mine in the nighttime. I could do no less than give them all the sustenance that I could provide to the total exhaustion of my energies.

When Mine are weaned, I must go away.

I paw and paw the earth beneath my muzzle. I ought not to whimper for these pups. These are the last of Mine from Bledsoe's great black and tan coonhound, the glorious dog who fucked all of us, who died in the great fire. My melancholy snout lies on the ground, and I whine for the pain in my hind leg and the loss.

Mine now gambol about. I revel in their smell! They are pretty! My exhausted, satisfied body happily gives them all. In the morning, at the sound of Its footfalls, I drag myself away, retreat to a hide from which I can observe Mine. Mine yip delightedly at Its approach.

One morning It brings meat and bread that Mine gleefully eat. I am happy. Mine are weaned. My teats dry up at the sight.

My broken leg does not heal. The rigors of whelping, nursing and escaping the fire have depleted me. I am resigned. My tail thumps the ground contentedly. This Mine, these of mine are my last ones. I am lighthearted, despite my misfortune, that Mine are weaned and well placed.

Robert Perron

Aches and Pains

Anne's phone, flat on the conference table, flickers. Her glance lingers, and when she looks up, five sets of opposing eyes have engaged hers. She veers back to work and says, "In my opinion, unit price must come in below four dollars."

Across the table, Ted says, "But that's not what I'm hearing if we want profit. Cost of goods alone—"

Outside the conference room, Ted says, "Everything okay, Anne?"

She holds up her phone. "The school nurse. Asshole should be dealing with this but he's MIA."

"Well, do what you have to," says Ted, "but would you call in later?"

Anne's halfway to Edgewood Middle when her phone buzzes and her ex's soft baritone drifts from the car's speakers. "My humble apologies, Annie. I just now got to my messages."

Anne says, "You are supposed to be—"

"I know, of course, but how can I predict that Brendon needs an early pickup?"

"Where exactly are you? Can you get to the school?"

"I'm afraid I'm on a job, out at the beach."

The car ahead stops for a yellow light, forcing Anne to jam her brakes. "Asshole," she says.

"Now, Annie, is that called for?"

Laugh or cry, take her choice. Anne wonders about the job site: the White Horse Tavern? Buddy's Cave? "Have you been drinking?" she asks. A stupid question, a rhetorical question, the answer the same no matter the level of toxicity.

"Annie, please, give me a break. You think I'd be drinking then picking up our child? I got a chance for some work." His sincerity flows from the speakers like honey on waffles, engendering a flash of remorse, until Anne remembers past declarations. His standing in front of her, lolling from side to side, lolling front to back, filling the foyer with brackish blasts of alcohol, saying *you're always accusing me. Why are you always accusing me?*

The school nurse says, "No temp. He complains of stomach cramps."

"What do you think?"

"Tylenol. If he keeps complaining, take him into emergency."

Tylenol. A possible trip to emergency. Brendon leans over his seat belt. "It really hurts, Mom." He has deep brown hair like her ex, a long face and snub nose, like the same.

"I'll run the pricing again when I get home," Anne tells Ted on speaker. "Okay, see you tomorrow."

Anne opens the front door to the narrow townhouse, living and kitchen down, two bedrooms up. *If he asks for a snack,* Anne tells herself, *or even looks at the kitchen, I swear I'll swat him.* But Brendon takes to the stairs. Anne follows his progress to the upper landing and into his bedroom, then settles at the kitchen table and opens her laptop.

Anne's ears perk to movement between bedroom and bathroom. She goes back to her spreadsheet.

For five minutes, Anne has heard no movement. She slips away from table and computer, slips up the stairs, and surveys the closed bathroom door. She allows another sixty seconds, then approaches and knocks. "Brendon, are you okay?"

Brendon's reply comes in high volume and a plaintive whine. "Mom."

Anne backs away, returns downstairs, returns to pricing. She's more sure than ever that the units must stay below four dollars.

The toilet flushes. Footsteps: bathroom to bedroom. Anne waits a minute and again ascends the stairs. She taps Brendon's door and it swings inward half a foot. Another tap and Anne inserts her head. Brendon lies on his bed on his back. He says, "I feel better, Mom."

Anne wants to ask if he washed his hands but forces herself to let the query pass. She says, "I don't mean to be nosy, Brendon. I just wanted to make sure you were okay."

"I think I'm okay now."

Anne stands in the doorway for a reassuring ten seconds. As she turns away, Brendon says, "Mom?"

She turns back.

"I'm sorry I dragged you out of work."

Anne waves her hand. "Oh Brendon. That's not a problem."

Sarah Freligh

Snow Baby

Her girl is disappearing, erased daily by the wan heat of a January sun. Her cold only child, the daughter she palmed into life out of snow and hope after the others were wrung out of her, little white dishrags. Afterward, the white space where she'd been stranded. Every day a blizzard in her brain, a windowless room until she flexed her fingers and built her girl. *Please come inside,* her husband begs her nightly. But no, not yet. Here is a pink hat, daughter. Can you see how I'm trying to save you?

NON-FICTION

Suzanne Altman

Autumn Stephens

Risk Management

A suspicious bra strap, and I almost missed the flight out; what can you do. What I did was fume in place, tapping my shoeless toe, rolling the balls of my eyes like a mime. Engine running, brakes locked: throttled. Didn't forward used to be a valid direction?
At least I'd thought to empty my pockets; only in a fairy tale would five metal disks have ticketed me for anything proximate to rapture. "Sorry, sorry," I had to tell my sons when I got home because dinner would be late and the world was burning and my bad. Optimism, these days that's like going barefoot or eating with your fingers, an indulgence for private atmospheres. The good news was, I said, no gunpowder on my palms.

Andrei Konchalovsky
Translated by Bryon MacWilliams

Mama

October 29, 1941. We are evacuating Moscow for Almaty, the former capital of Kazakhstan. Papa is driving us to the Tushino Airfield in a black GAZ-M1 *"Emka"* staff car. On the way we stop at the corner of Triumph Square near the Obraztsov Puppet Theater.

Grandfather and Grandmother walk out to the car, say goodbye. (They would remain in Moscow throughout the horrible winter of that year.)

They kiss me and Mama. They say goodbye to us as if it were forever.

I remember the plane, the inordinately tall boots of the machine gunner standing at the turret mount. In the skies above, Nazi fighters are circling, yet I, of course, cannot fathom the danger they present—don't even know what a war is.

Sergei Eisenstein was on the very same plane. I didn't know who he was, then.

I slept the entire flight, woke up in Almaty.

Once there we lived with great filmmakers in a so-called *Laureatnik*, a place for winners of the Stalin Prize (U.S.S.R. State Prize). I remember the tea urn, or *samovar*, at the end of the corridor. I remember Mama speaking English with Eisenstein, the director.

One of the most distressing losses from my life—stolen—is Eisenstein's screenplay for *Ivan Grozny* with an inscription, in English, to my mother, Nataliya Konchalovskaya. Later Mama would tell me how Eisenstein showed her his hooligan-like sketches of penises, each a different character. A sad-faced member. An insolent member. A melancholy member. An apathetic member.

During the war we didn't see Papa—the poet Sergei Mikhalkov, who wrote the lyrics for the Soviet national anthem—for half a year. Mama continued to translate poems, notably those of Mikhailo Stelmakh and Rubinstein. And life, it seemed to me, was happy—happy out of despair for the war.

In 1941, Mama was thirty-eight years old. She was young, very attractive. Only fourteen years earlier she had run away to America with another woman's husband. She and Aleksei Alekseevich Bogdanov—a merchant with the Amtorg Trading Corporation—fled to San Francisco via Vladivostok, then Japan. In those days it was possible to divorce by mail; before they had reached Vladivostok, Bogdanov received his divorce by telegram.

They married on the ship from Yokohama to San Francisco. In America they divorced and returned separately to the Soviet Union in 1933. Bogdanov was arrested immediately upon arrival and shot. If my mother hadn't divorced him the previous year, the same fate would have awaited her.

Her ensuing marriage to my father was somewhat strange. Unlike my father, she had a broad circle of friends and a broad education. Moreover, she was ten years older than his twenty-three years and had only just arrived from America. She not only spoke English fluently, but French.

Mama had always wanted a son but gave birth first to a daughter, Ekaterina. Later, while pregnant with me, she envisioned who I would become — my personality, my destiny.

She was an extremely passionate person. Because of my selfishness, I would realize that much too late. Like all children, I met her passion and love with demands and severity. A child always wants, but never gives.

Mama didn't give up on me, though. As I grew up, she began to share with me some of her thoughts. I listened to her patiently—she had a great deal she wanted to tell me — but only out of duty as a son. Mostly I was bored. My head was already swimming with other things: girls, parties, friends, movies.

By my mid-20s our relationship became more reciprocal, adult. Often she would tell me that she was writing a new story, or poem, then would say, "Hold on, let me read it to you."

The timing was always bad. I'd sit there, listening—all the time my hands roaming the most interesting places of the girl seated next to me.

When I left for America, I told Mama I wouldn't be coming back. We talked about it for a long time.

Tears filled her eyes. She said, "There's just no way you can do this."

Papa didn't have the foggiest idea, and she was afraid. When he found out, he was filled with resentment toward me.

At night, far from Russia, I placed three things on the headboard of the bed and felt at home: the small icon of Apostle Andrew the First-Called that sits in a black leather cover Mama sewed with her own hands (it formerly belonged to her grandfather, the painter Vasily Surikov), a prayer book she gave me, and a photograph of her. It seemed as if some kind of unknown energetic force emanated from these items. Their force sustained me, especially when I was feeling low.

When Mama and I sat in a car after the premiere of one of my films, she said, "You were right, you were right. I shouldn't have judged you. After all, at one point I up and left for America the exact same way."

Judith Lichtendorf

Untitled

My mother was tall and thin, angular even. She was close to being a chain smoker, drank a lot of black coffee during the day, and switched to scotch at night. She had no interest in clothes or cooking or decorating; she liked doing crossword puzzles and studying the bridge column in the newspaper, activities that didn't require lipstick or dressing up. She read and reread a thick leather-bound book with tissue paper pages that contained *The Collected Works of Somerset Maugham*. Her other favorite was a paperback, *The Penguin Collection of Great Poems,* and she would open it at random and read. She particularly liked Tennyson's poems, but any page was a good page, she said. Those two books stayed on the end table on her side of the couch, and mostly that's what she did, sit in her spot on the couch and read, except when we pestered her enough that she had to stop or it was time to prepare dinner.

Dinner was a can of tuna, plopped from the can into a bowl and stabbed a few times with a fork, green peppers cut into wedges, peeled raw carrots, hard boiled eggs sliced in half, rye bread and butter. *That's enough for dinner,* she would say. Sometimes my father said, *Let's add some nuts to the situation*, and he'd open a can of Planters Fancy Cocktail Mix and dump them in a bowl. My mother would say, *Good, nuts are protein.* Dinner variations: cans of salmon. Brisling sardines. Wedges of iceberg lettuce. Celery sticks.

In those days a new convenience was frozen white fish which you could buy in supermarkets. So every once in a while she would announce, *Tonight I am going to cook*, and she would make fish. She would come home with the frozen package, tear its paper wrapper off, put the frozen block of fish in the kitchen sink and run hot water over it until it had thawed enough for her to be able to pry apart the fillets and spread them out on a cookie sheet. She put a few little dabs of butter on top of the still half-iced fish pieces and shook McCormick Paprika over them until they were coated orange. Then the fillets went into the oven at 350 degrees where they lay until dinnertime. She would scrape them off the cookie sheet with a spatula and place them on a serving dish with some lemon wedges cut up on one end. When she brought this plate to the dinner table, my dad would always look at it, pause, and say, *Just the way I like it—cremated.*

We had a maid, Edna, who came three times a week. She did the laundry, cleaned the apartment and sometimes when we begged, my mom would ask Edna to stay late and make us fried chicken for dinner. That was a great meal. The only one who didn't eat it was my mom. *I don't eat fowl,* she said. *Fowl is foul.* That was her kind of line.

My sisters and I worried about the same thing, who did mom love best. This was a constant subject of intense interest to us, and we would pester my mother so often that she would sometimes just groan and refuse to respond. *Stop it,* she would say. *Find something else to bother me with.*

But we couldn't stop, there was nothing else we needed to know. *Who do you love the best,* we asked, again and again. We would try to trap her into revealing her heart.

If we were all on a boat and it began to sink and you only had one life preserver who would you save, Ellen or Fran or me?

86

I would save you all.

But if you couldn't. If you only had one life preserver and you absolutely had to pick.

I wouldn't pick, I would save all of you.

But if you couldn't.

I would find a way. Stop asking, it's a ridiculous question, I would save all three of you.

But what if we had all fallen down into the subway tracks and the train was coming and she only had time to pull one of us out. If a truck lost control and was barreling towards us and she could only push one of us to safety. If a starving lion. A lunatic with a knife. Fallen into an icy lake and she could hold a rope out to only one of us in time to save—which life? Which daughter? Who did she love best?

I would find a way. I would save you all.

But if you couldn't.

I would be able to. Somehow I would find a way.

But if you couldn't.

I want to read now, stop bothering me. See if you can stand on your head, she would suggest, and roll her eyes.

Tsaurah Litzky

"As Ye Sow, So Shall Ye Reap"

When I was a little girl I once asked my mother if she believed in heaven. She didn't answer me right away. She puckered her lips in a way I had come to know meant she was thinking.

"I'll tell you just what my father told me," she finally said. He told me, "If there is such a place, no one ever came back to tell me about it." Then she added, "Here in America anyone can believe what they want. That's good, and we Jews don't believe in heaven or hell. Maybe some people may have made those places up because they were afraid to trust their own consciences. I don't really know, but always trust your conscience," she said. "If it tells you something is wrong, don't do it!"

Many times in my adult life, I have learned how valuable this advice was, so good for avoiding strife and sorrow. I remember the time I went to bed with by friend Harriet's husband. He was very persistent, very attractive. A voice inside me, my conscience, kept telling me, *No, No, it's wrong, she's your friend,* but I succumbed anyhow. It was terrible, like having sex with a dental drill. I kept seeing her face. I was not surprised to hear a year later they were divorcing. It turned out he was very persistent with many of her friends, but that still didn't excuse me.

I can't say my mother is my conscience. I realize as a supposed adult, I bear responsibility for what goes on in my head. I can say so many of the things my mother told me linger in my memory. She comes to me when I don't expect her. Sometimes she tells me to hold on, sometimes she tells me to let go.

The first book my mother ever bought me was from Fingerhoff's Used Book Store, around the corner from where we lived with my grandparents in Brownsville, East New York.

The Fingerhoffs and my mother were friends. She loved to read. She was always visiting the store with me in tow. The Fingerhoffs suggested *Aesop's Fables.* They said it was a beautiful book that would teach me about life. It was published in 1925 by Whitman and Company, a long-gone Chicago publisher. Each fable was accompanied by an exquisite color drawing by one Joseph E. Dash. He was obviously a great lover of animals because of the way he made them come alive on the page.

I was five and couldn't read much. I would sit on my mother's knees, holding the book in front of us, she would read it to me.

My mother's absolute favorite fable was, *The Fox and The Stork,* which appears on page 200. Its entirety is quoted below:

At one time the Fox and the Stork were on visiting terms and seemed very good friends so the Fox invited the stork to dinner, and for a joke put nothing before her but some soup in a very shallow dish. This the Fox could easily lap up but the stork could only wet the end of her long bill in it, and left the meal as hungry as when she began. "I am sorry," said the Fox, "the soup is not to your liking."

"Pray do not apologize," said the Stork. "I hope you will return this visit and come dine with me soon." So a day was appointed when the Fox should visit the Stork; but when they were seated at the table, all that there was for dinner was contained in a very long-necked jar with a

88

narrow mouth, in which the Fox could not insert his snout, so all the Fox could manage to do was to lick the outside of the jar.

"*I will not apologize for the dinner,*" *said the Stork.*

As ye sow, so shall ye reap read the words at the bottom of the page. My mother read this fable to me many, many times. She was always trying to teach me to take responsibility for my actions. When I stole a Hershey bar from the corner grocery, I had to return it with an apology. When I made a mess in my room by not picking up after myself, I had to stay in my room until I cleaned it up.

Now seventy years later, I'm still not good at picking up after myself, but I'm better than I was. I try hard, very hard, not to create messes by my actions or reactions to others. I know I have no time to waste. I still have *Aesop's Fables.* It rests in a place of honor on my bedside table. I refer to it often, one of the many great treasures my mother gave me.

Tzynya Pinchback

While sorrow trickled from you like a spring

you mixed a Lidocaine salve for my burnt skin and placed a basin of tepid water and lavender oil on the bed where I lay curled, head nesting in the crook of my arm, as if repentant. You hummed the same song about divine grace, your faith unwavering as you did this work. At 69, your hands steady, you pressed firm on my groin, pulling taut the adhesive tape to undress the wound. One by one, you soaked paper towels in the sweet-smelling water, washed and patted dry my falling-away skin. When I winced, drawing my hands into fists, you slowed your pace and reminded me to expose the wound, allow it to breathe—*every living thing needs oxygen.* You, standing at the window, clumps of paper towels like wilted peonies in your grasp, whispered, *I wish it was me,* as if spoken full out the words were embers and my body the sagebrush. But then you laughed. Said I was too young to have cancer *and* old lady hands—your and your mother's hands. Small soft lines that carry the perfume of cinnamon and lime long after the last mound of dough has been rolled out and folded around apples for pie. Slender fingers that pull plant from soil, leaf from stem, but just as easily smooth hair knots into lush coils. You are right. These hands have never been new. We enter this world already holding our mother's stories.

Heather Haldeman

"The Dwindles"

My sister and I are meeting a new crew this morning at The Jewish Home. The "Hospice Team." This is the last rung on our mother's care cycle. We are seated around a beige-colored table that doubles for dining; it feels like a business meeting. And it is. The business is that our 91 year-old mother is dying.

Present are a chaplain, two social workers, Mom's hospice nurse, and Josie, her floor nurse. My sister, April, and I are seated side-by-side. We discuss medication. Morphine is at the ready.

"Parkinson's," the hospice nurse says, "is tough to predict. There is no time line. We just know that she's declining."

It's often called "the dwindles," the chaplain adds, soft with empathy.

"So," one of the social workers says, pulling out her laptop and giving a smile. "Tell us about your mother."

"Oh my god," April laughs and turns to me.

"She's basically a cross between Carol Channing and Phyllis Diller who thinks she's Marilyn Monroe," I say. "Our mother had three husbands. For her, it's always been about a man."

The group's eyes grow wide. The chaplain laughs. "Fabulous! What a character."

"But now that Bernie, her most recent 'boyfriend' passed," April makes air quotes around boyfriend, "it's like flatline for Mom. There's no man in her life. Or even a potential one!"

"You should have seen her when she first arrived three years ago," Josie pipes in. "She never left her room without full make-up and false eyelashes. She had so many pairs, sometimes when I'd leave her room, I'd have an eyelash stuck to my pant leg!"

"At mealtimes, we put her next to Bernie," Josie adds. "She'd be fine until Ruth would show up and vie for Bernie's attention."

"Mom called Ruth the 'bitch from Brooklyn-before-it-got-good.'" I add.

"Then there was the issue with food," I turned to my sister. "Remember when poor Rose, seated to Mom's right at mealtimes, was losing weight and Mom was gaining?"

"Mom was stealing her food," April laughs.

"Wow," replies the other social worker, tapping away at her laptop. As mom would say, her eyes were on stems. "Really?" she asks. "She didn't!"

"Trust me," April says. "She did."

"Don't forget the tattoo she got at 85," I say. "She always wanted one."

"This is quite a story," she says, back on her laptop. "I wish I'd met her before now."

"And then, there's the time she escaped her room at Sunrise Senior Living before she came here," April says. "They found her with her then-boyfriend 'the doctor.' They'd both used their walkers for a field trip to the liquor store at the corner to buy wine and Advil."

"What about when she fell at Sunrise and the handsome paramedics came?" April now mimics her voice: "I'd fall again to be carried off by two hunky men."

By now, the hospice nurse has stopped taking notes. The social worker finishes capturing this last tale of Mom's. The room grows quiet.

"She's a survivor," I say, looking at April. "And she's not going to go down easy."

"Hell no," April nods.

One of the social workers tells us about a conversation she'd overheard between two residents on the second floor. "They don't let you die here," they'd agreed with each other.

"It's this desire for our caregivers to make our residents better," the chaplain weighs in. "But in your mother's case, she's not going to get better, so we are making it comfortable for her to …" she trails off.

"Everyone loves your mother," Josie interrupts, looking at my sister and me.

I was reminded of the caregiver who'd stopped by Mom's room last week. I'd been seated next to her wheelchair waiting for her to wake.

"I'd been having some problems in my marriage," she told me quietly. "Your Mom, she listened. She gave me advice. She helped me get through it, and it's okay now…" She'd rubbed Mom's shoulder as she sat asleep in her wheelchair, then she leaned down close to Mom's ear. "We love you, Marilyn."

At the time, I'd looked up at the ceiling to hold back the tears.

"It's ok," she'd told me. "We're all crying about losing her."

April's voice brought me back. "Mom's got a sixth sense, an intuitive power. Almost feral," she tells the group. She looks over at me and her voice lowers, filled with emotion. "Heather and I miss her." She pauses to compose herself. "That quick wit and perfect answer to a situation. She could just call it, you know? She had a saying for everything."

I feel wistful. Mom may have been flawed like the rest of us, but I loved her unconditionally. And though she's still alive, she's not really present anymore.

"She used to say, 'I'd rather be happy than right,'" I offer.

"Or," April adds, "He's looks a lot taller when he stands on his money!"

The room fills with laughter again.

Mom's sayings have a way of doing that.

* My mother passed away peacefully in the early morning hours the day after I wrote this essay.

eve packer

washes
> —*mon, 7/23/18: 4:45 pm*

you drop the *daily news.*
put down yr tea.
you have heard a sound,
a repeated sound
harsh, unyielding, bones knocking
air knocking struggle—
death rattle—

you hold her—
tell her we all love her,
and you name our names,
hear yr voice singing
easy living—her and your father's
favorite billie holiday tune,
the only time they ever got
along, its all right you say,
and hear your voice:
she is having such a hard time
with breath—
we love you................
you can let go—

she's gone

        the skin turns yellow,
        hairs sprout from chin,
        the cheekbones, rise,
        the cheeks sink—

no matter:
as you hold yr mother
thru last breath
 something, someone,
sun thru shade on wall,
something, someone
washes thru

the dna in every cell
realigns, like child-
birth, sun reflected
thru shade
on wall

something, someone

when you hold her
thru last breath, something, someone,
sun reflected thru shade
on the wall, washes through you

when you hold her
thru last breath, like child-
birth, sun reflected
thru shade
on the wall, something, someone, washes thru you

you can't hold or touch it, but
every cell realigns,
a change

something, someone,
sun reflected thru shade
on the wall
something, someone
washes thru
you

Alisa A. Gaston

Her Icelandic Storybook

She tells me I can do it. Wrap her up in a blanket covered in blue owls, and catapult her to the crusty, circular floor hanging in the night sky. When I ask her why, she seems surprised. "So the mean ones won't get me."

*

I think I can convince her that instead, I'll fly her to Snjóland, where mothers leave babies in carriages on the sidewalks. Babies' lungs fill with crisp resilience in this place of fiords and steaming lakes that heal afflictions. I can't bring myself to tell her that the mean ones within her body will follow wherever she travels.

*

My girl thinks of soft, white dirt. Thinks it will comfort her, take the place of the mean ones. I want to bury them in the moon craters. I want to reshape myself into a particle, enter her skin, swim within her cerebral circulation, find the mean ones in her brain, and dislodge them with a clean icicle from a pure glacier. I would use precision. I would work around her optic nerves with care where the mean ones have planted, cut them from the tissue, strap them on my back, then leave her body. Her brain would heal, and she would never again be threatened with blindness.

*

When I hold her in my arms, she tells me that I am her "best darling." I visualize us in Snjóland, imagine the fishing lands, and the smell of black sand beaches. She tells me the story where the baby bear puts a box on his head and tells the mama bear that he's flying to the moon. I tell her I'll take her where we will see white foxes and hear the cracking and crunching from reindeer walking. I will cover her with her blue-owl blanket while she stretches across earth, air, fire, and water.

*

"I can't send you to the moon," I confess. "It is as dark and lonely as my heart without you."

*

I want the threat of hot lava more than the threat of disease. At least with the volcano, we might run from danger as one, or we might fade into the toxic gas. I remember when she was three and asked, "Mommy, will we die together?" "Most likely not," I told her. Later, "Mommy, when we die together, can we hold hands?"

*

We will eradicate the mean ones in her brain when science catches up. For now, I will take her where we will drink beautiful water. I'll say it's the moon. Put your little hand into mine, my best darling, and I will take you to a safer place of light and darkness.

Jennifer Case

Plagiocephaly

In moderate cases, like that of my infant son, one cheek pops out and one side of the forehead protrudes. The ear, too, has shifted—migrating half an inch forward—as the neurosurgeon shows us, his five gloved fingers holding my son's head still, while my son grins a two-toothed grin, silly and bubbling and oblivious.

It isn't serious. Or terribly serious, at least. His skull hasn't fused prematurely, and his brain has room to grow. The largest drawbacks: Eyeglasses may wobble. Helmets for sports may not fit. He may develop jaw issues and TMJ. He may, as a teenager, grow his hair out, self-conscious.

They recommend helmet therapy. "They" being the neurosurgeon, in our room for five minutes, followed by the orthotic technician who says, "Don't feel pressured." Two sample helmets sit on a table. One in camo. One bright pink. Each was molded to a single child, designed to apply pressure to the already round side, forcing the flattened spot to expand into the "unobstructed" zone.

"It's a conspiracy," I whisper to my husband, because I've perhaps read too much. The orthotic helmet industry burgeoned immediately after the back-to-sleep movement, when parents, fearful of SIDS, stopped placing their infants on their bellies, and babies' soft skulls began to flatten against the mattresses of cribs. Our ways of childrearing had changed, with physical effects on children's bodies. Helmets: a means to recreate a cultural or evolutionary norm.

Not that anything is inherently normal. One of the orthotic technician's cheek bones bulges, and the right side of his chin dwarfs the other. I wonder if he suffered a concussion from football: the impact of body on body breaking his nose. I expect he barrels through life, collecting a helmet-selling commission, and that's why he doesn't note my hesitations. Though maybe it wasn't football. Maybe his head, too, had flattened in infancy. Maybe that's why, after he's taken the scan, and said one diagonal of our son's skull is more than a centimeter shorter than the other, and I ask what we should do, he says, "If it were my child, I'd put him in a helmet."

In MRIs, the human visual cortex lights up at the sight of symmetry. Asymmetry, on the other hand, elicits disgust. When my son was two months old, his flat spot most pronounced, I'd sometimes look at him and realize, even as his mother, that he was not exactly an attractive child. I'd bring him to daycare, or wheel him at the park, and know that others noticed it, too. They paused at his lopsided, parallelogram-shaped skull before shifting their attention to praise his quick smile.

Our insurance company considers orthotic helmets cosmetic. Sometimes they deny the claims. I want this to mean something: that the physical doesn't matter, that people will see past my son's head shape, that a misshapen head does not warrant a $2,000 helmet, and that the helmet industry, like plastic surgery, like Botox, like make-up, like high fashion, like photoshopped profiles in glossy magazines, marks something shallow, uncomfortable, and unbecoming of our species.

Though maybe I'm just defensive. Sometimes my son rubs his flat spot against the back of his high chair or the mattress of his bed. Back and forth, rapidly, as if finding the place where the two parallel planes slide perfectly together. It delights me: his delight in the way it fits, and for a moment I forget what I've read about other cultures that modified infants' skulls. The Olmecs and Mayans, Caribbeans and Chinooks. Certain bourgeois communities in Switzerland and France. They used cradleboards and planks, or bonnets and headbands, to produce everything from cone heads, to two-lobed heads, to flattened foreheads or flattened napes. When my son rubs his flat spot against his high chair and grins, I think, *If our culture were more appreciative of asymmetry, my son's head would be a sign of beauty, too.*

Of course, cultural conceptions of beauty affect quality of life. Of course, self-esteem could be an issue. Of course, culture teaches us who is attractive, and that affects mating rituals. Sitting in the orthotic technician's office, I lower my nose to my son's hair and imagine him in high school, in college, probably pimply and wearing glasses. I imagine him nursing heartbreak, touching his misaligned ears. This in the end is what gets me. I want him to experience love.

Devin Overman

It's Nothing Like the Apocalypse, I'm Sure

He's reading now, but a few moments ago my son was a demon. Writhing limbs, guttural noises, sharp talons aiming for delicate parts. My hair is out of the way, so he grabs for my neck, but I dodge in time. If angels can fall, perhaps so can a cherub, so perhaps he is one, with his soft cheeks, long lashes, and dead eyes.

I work my exorcism. I am not a trained priest, so I must make do. As he and I enter our seventh year together, I have picked up a few tricks of the trade from other child-demon mother-exorcists, but most have come from my own experience. Keep your hair back. Don't be too fond of your clothes, especially the necklines, and always, always guard your face.

My words aren't always effective, and today is another day they fail me. I regret choosing French over Latin in school. As we battle, I search for the source, the moment my smart, letter-obsessed, wobbly boy was exchanged with a changeling. In the span of a second, my mind distracted, my demon finds a gap in my armor and strikes.

The scratch follows the line of a tear from the middle of my eye to the apple of my cheek. It is superficial, no blood shed this time, but it is enough. I disengage with him to check my wound. This time, he senses the change in mood. I incite all number of things in him. I'm told it's only me with whom he acts this way.

When I return, he's reciting Arthur episode titles on his tablet. His limbs are in repose; he sings as the next season loads.

Only a century or so ago, my child's behavior would have been cause to summon an actual priest. He might not have survived to his seventh year. Today, the news reports that not much has changed except the priest part, and despite the reddening faux tear, I am thankful again for the village I have amassed that helps tame my boy's demon and help us both understand that it's not supernatural at all.

He's different, and he trusts only me with his terror.

Elizabeth Newdom

Oz, the Great and Powerful

The *pop-pop* of gunfire pierces the air of my young son's room as he drifts off to sleep. He lies in a crescent shape, clutching his blankie, and I am thinking of Trayvon Martin, Syrian refugees, and students in Parkland, Florida. Moments ago I was singing "Frere Jacques."

Pop-pop. Pop-pop-pop...pop.

Every Wednesday is the same. I put my boy to bed to the backdrop of gunfire, and I wonder if it penetrates his consciousness. I wonder, too, if we should have bought this yellow house up on the hill, the one I adored for its historic-modern charm. The one within a mile from the firing range.

Every Sunday, I can sit and listen to the wind chime's melodic chant. I can rest with a chipped mug of coffee while my boy reads another of his *I Survived* books on the couch. Among his favorites are *I Survived The Battle of Gettysburg, I Survived The Great Chicago Fire, I Survived the Sinking of The Titanic.*

Every night, he reads to me for 10 minutes, often ending his day with one of these heart-pounding tales of tragedy and triumph. I try to focus on the triumph part, so I can justify his obsession. Is it rewarding to read about survival night after night? Does he need the resounding message that sad stories end well?

When I was a girl, I, too, sought shelter in tales of fantasy. Each spring, the honeysuckle vines returned and covered the chain-link fence between my garage and the neighbor's yard, where I'd run and hide. The aroma of flowers and pungent nectar enveloped my senses, transporting me someplace magical like Narnia or Oz. I'd plant myself, sheltered from the storm whipping inside my tornadic house, counting down the minutes until I could safely assume the Wicked Witch was dead.

But the tornado that whisked Dorothy away to Oz was hardly real. My boy's stories of true disasters make my heart ache and nerves splinter.

Pop-pop. Pop-pop-pop...pop.

I cringe while taking his leftover milk and crackers, a storytime ritual, down to the kitchen, imaging the Legos strewn across the floor are gun shells from some Civil War battle outside our door.

I boil water for tea and settle into the couch with my laptop, envisioning the book I could write called *I Survived Parenthood.* It would start with all the ways we're stuck behind the curtain, like the Wizard, shading our children from one terrible truth or another. And I wonder how long I can keep up the act.

As my boy approaches eight, he still believes in Santa, the Easter Bunny, and the Tooth Fairy. He doesn't know where babies come from, thinks grandparents only die in bad movies, and if the seventh grader on our block hadn't opened his big mouth, my boy would still be blissfully unaware that Kylo Ren kills Han Solo.

Knowing if and when to unveil the truth is difficult. On the one hand, my son shows such maturity. He takes out the trash, feeds our cat, Sage, and completes his homework without a fuss. He wants to know if ghosts are real and if, in fact, he is Jewish or Christian. But at other times, it's clear he is only seven. He will leave the fridge door open, forget to look both ways, and ask me to brush his teeth. He is still afraid to ride a bike without training wheels or swim without a life vest. He still wants to be tucked in at night.

Pop-pop. Pop-pop-pop...pop.

Against what are people arming themselves, I wonder? But I pull up the daily news on my iPhone and remember. If I am the Wizard, then my son is the Scarecrow, the Tin Man, and the Lion, all rolled into one.

Someday he'll grasp that *I Survived September 11* was an actual event, and that the Pentagon is a mere 50 miles from our house on the hill. He'll discover that *I Survived the Joplin Tornado* is based on a true disaster, and I will tell him about the tornado we dodged in Atlanta that spring—and how I stayed up all night listening for the whistling train.

But for now, I will keep singing "Frere Jacques" and be grateful he doesn't ask what that noise is in the distance.

Heidi Czerwiec

Like

"He looks just like you!"

I hear this a lot. Wyatt and I share the same dark eyes and long lashes, fine but abundant pin-straight dark brown hair. But Wyatt, while most definitely my son, is not my biological child. Wyatt and I share the same coloring because his birthmother and I do—both short, curvy women of Eastern European heritage (her, Czech; me, Polish), dark eyes, dark hair. Whether consciously or not, she may have considered this likeness when considering me to mother this son.

And people comment on this likeness all the time. I always correct them, add the asterisk, try to honor his history and assert his own independent appearance. I reply, "I know! But you should see a picture of his birthmother—he really looks like her, down to the dimpled cheek and chin, the shape of his nose and mouth." Despite, or possibly because of this assertion, most are quick to add, "Oh no, I'd definitely recognize him as your son, anywhere!" I would too.

I know they're being kind, maybe covering for their surprise or embarrassment from assuming he's my child. But he *is* my child, even though he doesn't have my thick build, my Czerwiec nose. What's even weirder is when people claim the same resemblance, *he looks like you,* to my husband, whose Nordic Nelson genes—blond barrel-chested folk with wintry eyes and solid skulls—bear no expression in our son.

Our son. Everyone wants to assert it. They want us to know that *they* know we go together. Perhaps it's a throwback to earlier adoptions, the attempt to pretend parentage, a pretense to be preserved at all costs—seal the records, swear family to secrecy, move towns—all to establish credibility. Perhaps because so many of these children were wrested from unwed mothers, society acquired an interest in this pretense to divert attention from an uncomfortable truth, a mother with a legitimate claim to her child deemed illegitimate so that the child could be placed with a "real" family of whom society could comfortably approve. But that attitude, at its heart, was unkind, and I believe our acquaintances mean to be kind.

But is this pretense still necessary? I don't feel threatened by acknowledging the adoption, don't feel it makes our family any less legitimate, or Wyatt any less our son. I want to preserve and honor both his own separate history and how it intersects with ours. I don't feel the need to paper over it and hope nothing leaks through.

So yes, I'll confess—something in me is pleased when people see we go together. It goes beyond looks. Certain gestures, like the way I shrug while lifting my palms and scrunching my mouth. How I twist my lips, raise my eyebrows, and cut my eyes to the side to indicate I'm teasing. I've seen these gestures mirrored in him. And behaviors, both good—thanking people politely—and bad, like his (my) too-easy frustration when a new skill isn't instantly easy. He's even picking up my penchant for swearing.

Even further: I'm a perfume collector, and Wyatt is irresistibly attracted to my many bottles and samples, loves sniffing their contents with me. While he's not a connoisseur of the orientals and leather scents I prefer, he's partial to florals, orange blossom and jasmine, in particular. He often pleads with me for a spritz. And I often grant it. We choose a bottle—his tastes are young, and he's often swayed by a flashy flaçon or brightly-colored juice—say, *Seville à L'Aube*, an orange fluid in a dramatic octagonally-cut glass bottle. I uncap it and spray him lightly, but only on the arms since I don't think the sensitive skin of his neck can tolerate it. I spray myself too, and we enjoy the greeny-orange blossom scent as I rub my arms against his, perfuming him, marking him with my scent, like an animal, making him mine.

Nancy Vona

Plight of the Queen Bee

One morning in August, my husband enters the kitchen of our summer house on Cape Cod. He tells me that he has been living a lie, that he has been anxious and unhappy for years, if not decades.

He remains depressed for nearly a year. The depression is a tsunami, a force that drags our entire family under until we gasp and sputter for breath and beg for mercy. My husband is functioning at his high level job, but at home he is withdrawn, sometimes in tears. Our marriage has always consisted of my doing most of the work in our relationship: initiating difficult conversations, tolerating his anger and silence. Now the anger and silences increase in duration, frequency, and intensity.

While he is at work and the boys are at school, I search "what to do when a spouse doesn't want to have sex" and "what to do when your spouse is depressed and withdrawn" on Google. In the past, women consulted the Bible, their mothers, tarot cards, wise women. Google is my oracle, my wise crone. I pretend everything is "fine," sending out Christmas cards and posting happy photos of our dogs and boys on Facebook. On the outside, our life is a suburban paradise of a beautiful house, well-behaved teenagers, playful dogs. There are snakes even in paradise.

Life goes on. I shop, cook, wash and fold laundry, make beds, clean. Make appointments for the pediatrician, the dentist, the veterinarian. Fill out forms for Boy Scouts, photography camp, swim team, volleyball, saxophone lessons, band practice, rowing league, high school and middle school registration. I drive the boys to their activities, take our three dogs to the vets. I try to write. I am barely holding on.

My husband tells me he doesn't love himself and that he needs to learn to love himself before he can love me. "Where does that leave me?" I ask. He doesn't reply.

"Where do you see yourself in five years?" I ask. "Am I in the picture?"

"I want to be happy in five years," he says. He doesn't say, I want to be happy with you.

In the midst of my loneliness and isolation, I tend to my honeybees. The bees are my lifeline, the one thing I am doing right. After a Massachusetts winter of record-breaking cold temperatures, many experienced beekeepers lost their hives. I have only been beekeeping for three years, but all five of my colonies survived the winter.

Winter skips right to summer. Under a cloudless blue sky, in the back yard where the air is sweet with the scent of blueberry, strawberry, and lilac blossoms, I care for the honeybees and breathe through my uncertainty and anxiety. The bees are housed in clean white Langstroth hive boxes, nestled among goldenrod, hyssop, calendula and borage.

I inspect each hive to make sure it is queenright—that the queen is alive and healthy. I light the smoker with newspaper and wood chips. The flame leaps up, hot and steady, and sears my gloved hands. I puff smoke in the hive entrance to calm the bees. A peek under the inner cover reveals thousands of workers—all females; they do the heavy work of the hive.

Beekeeping allows me moments of grace, the opportunity to be here now. In spite of my sadness, life goes on, and is going on right outside my doorstep. The workers tend to the queen, forage for pollen and nectar, turn nectar into honey like alchemy, nurse the eggs and larvae, clean the hive. The indifference of the natural world is strangely reassuring to me. The creatures around me do not care whether I break down in tears in the produce section of the local Whole Foods store or whether my marriage fails.

When I open one of the hives, I hear a roaring sound. The queen in this hive is several years old. She is failing. As she ages, chaos erupts in the hive. The worker bees are confused and belligerent. In a situation with an aging queen, sometime the entire hive population will abandon the hive. Sometimes the workers will kill her and raise a new queen.

I am that failing queen. Several months into menopause, with a marriage in crisis, I am floundering, my body untouched and incapable of producing new life. My house is like that hive body: beautiful and tidy on the outside, but within the four walls the balance is askew, dangerously so.

One of my beekeeper friends inspects this hive and tells me that I need to replace the queen with an emerging queen from another hive. "Take this frame," he says, showing me a frame of brood, eggs, and special larvae that are being raised as queens, "and put it in that hive"—pointing to the hive with the failing queen.

In the 80 degree heat, in my bee suit, I hesitate. Sweat drips down my face. Salt stings my eyes.

I cannot kill that queen. Not today. Instead, I close up the hive and walk away.

Turning

A friend wrote today, sent me a poem in which she ruminated on Tina Turner. Her words transported me to high school days when the singer's "Two People," one of the songs from the *Break Every Rule* album, was a favorite. I had my worst crush then, on a boy named Alex. We liked each other but were both too shy (or scared) to ever move beyond friendship. I'd sometimes see him when I played basketball at the fitness club his father managed. I used to go there to play pick-up games with men, who had a different style of play than the way my coaches instructed. "Run the play, run the play," my coaches yelled from the sidelines, meaning we should only shoot when each player ran a specific pattern to confuse the defense. We weren't supposed to shoot unless we were open, or unguarded. The men at the gym played a simple game. Get open, then take the shot. They were faster, took more shots. Missed baskets weren't tragedy. Get open again, take another shot.

In the off-season, when I wasn't confined to someone else's rules, I went to the gym where I played faster and took more shots to improve my offense. While showering in the locker room, I'd sometimes hear "Two People." Turner sang of "two" not three or four or five. It had to be Alex she meant, as she sang about people taking care of each other, I thought. My sixteen-year old self thought.

After I read my friend's poem, I googled the lyrics. My forty-seven-year-old self saw the words differently than I when I was sixteen and my estrogen level was surging and I ached for feelings I didn't yet know. According to recent lab results, my body is now in what one medical website termed "ovarian failure." I'm not surprised. Eighteen months ago, which was about three weeks after my last breakup, all feelings of sexual attraction came to a screeching halt. I still had profiles on dating sites but any time a man wrote to me, I had a visceral negative reaction. I clenched my jaw and fists, pulled my shoulders together, and shuddered. I knew LonelyDad427 anticipated a different response when he emailed me with the opening line, "Hey, sexy." At the time, I thought I wasn't ready to date again. But now, all these months later, I still feel the same.

"Are you okay?" Mom asked when I told her what the blood tests revealed. "Women sometimes get depressed when they know they aren't fertile anymore."

I felt like I was supposed to answer, "Yes, I'm depressed," but I didn't because it's not how I feel. I feel calm. I feel free. I feel like I'm playing by my own rules now. The romance has fallen by the wayside, but my love has multiplied. Today I read a moving email from a friend. I spent an hour on the phone catching up with another. My writing partner and I plotted together. I thought of Turner's lyrics about how people protect each other during storms. "Two People" doesn't mean "him and me" anymore.

Is it any wonder that my heart feels fuller now than any of the times I let myself sky dive, arms spread outward, hurling fast into some kind of passionate coupling that was anything but safe? Is it any wonder that I feel more like myself now than when the hormones in my body kept shouting at me, "Run the play, run the play?"

CONTRIBUTORS' NOTES

Allison Adair's poems have appeared or are forthcoming in *American Poetry Review, Best American Poetry* (2018), *Best New Poets, Boston Review, North American Review, Pleiades,* and *ZYZZYVA,* among other journals; and have received the Pushcart Prize (2019), the *Florida Review* Editors' Award, the Orlando Prize, and first place in the Fineline Competition from *Mid-American Review.* Originally from central Pennsylvania, Allison now lives in Boston, where she teaches at Boston College and Grub Street.

Julia C. Alter is living, writing, and raising a toddler in Burlington, Vermont. Recent poems can be found in *Rogue Agent, SWWIM Every Day*, and *CALYX.*

Suzanne Altman is an artist, teacher, and lecturer in art history. Visit Suzanne on Instagram at @artworkshudson, and on her website, www.suealtmanart.com.

Catherine Maryse Anderson is a poet, essayist, equity and inclusion facilitator, and educator in Portland, Maine. Her first manuscript, "Black Enough," explores transracial parenting and racial awakening as an adoptive and biological parent of Black and biracial sons. Her current project, "Skinny Dipped," is a combination of the written and spoken word, exploring grief in many forms, and the gifts within. She shares her poetry and stories at mamacandtheboys.com.

Stephane Angelini has degrees from Boston University and Suffolk University, and she lives on the North Shore of Massachusetts. Her poetry cycle "Death Always Went With the Territory" can be seen online in the current issue of *The American Journal of Poetry,* and she also has publications in *Third Wednesday, Ascent,* and the upcoming Fall edition of *Brittle Star.*

Jane Attanucci is a retired college professor. Her poems have appeared in *The Aurorean, Bird's Thumb, Off the Coast, The Pittsburgh Poetry Review* and *Third Wednesday,* among others. She won the Barbara Bradley Prize from the New England Poetry Club in 2014. Her chapbook, *First Mud,* was released by Finishing Line Press (2015). She lives in Cambridge, Massachusetts, close to her grandchildren.

Deborah Bacharach is the author of *After I Stop Lying* (Cherry Grove Collections, 2015). Her work has appeared in *Pembroke, Arts & Letters, The Southampton Review,* and *The Texas Review,* among many others. She is an editor, teacher and tutor in Seattle. Find out more about her at DeborahBacharach.com.

Lauren Banks is a poet and mother living in Virginia. She works in HIV/AIDS housing policy and is pursuing her Masters in Divinity. She has been published in *Tinderbox Poetry Journal* and holds an MFA from Vermont College of Fine Arts.

Carol Barrett holds doctorates in both clinical psychology and creative writing. She coordinates the Creative Writing Certificate Program at Union Institute & University. Her books include *Calling in the Bones,* which won the Snyder Prize from Ashland Poetry Press, *Drawing Lessons* from Finishing Line Press, and *Pansies,* a work of creative nonfiction, from Sonder Press. Her poems have appeared in *JAMA, Poetry International, Poetry Northwest, The Women's Review of Books,* and many other venues.

Janet Barry is a musician, poet, and photographer, with poems published in numerous journals and anthologies, most recently *Mom Egg Review, Third Wednesday, Clementine,* and *Radius Lit.* Her photography has appeared in publications such as *Off the Coast, Around Concord,* and *Parenthesis,* and she has received multiple Pushcart nominations, as well as a Best of the Net award from *BiLines.* Janet hold degrees in organ performance and poetry.

Rachel Barton, poet, writing coach, and member of the Calyx Editorial Collective, edits *Willawaw Journal*, and co-chairs Willamette Writers on the River. Find her poems in *Hubbub, Whale Road Review, Cloudbank,* and other journals. *Out of the Woods* was released in 2017. *Happiness Comes* is forthcoming from Dancing Girl Press.

Jennifer Jackson Berry is the author of *The Feeder* (YesYes Books, 2016), as well as the chapbook *Bloodfish* (Seven Kitchens Press, 2019). She lives in Pittsburgh, Pennsylvania.

Mary Bonina is the author of *My Father's Eyes : A Memoir*. Her poetry collections include *Living Proof, Clear Eye Tea*, and the chapbook *Lunch In Chinatown*. " Grace in the Wind," a poetry collaboration with composer Paul Sayed, premiered at Longy School of Music of Bard College. A Board member of the Writer's Room of Boston and a VCCA fellow, Bonina received a VCCA-France residency in September 2018.

Marietta Brill's poetry, essays, and reviews can be found in *Thrush Poetry Journal, hyperallergic.com, About Place Journal/Rewilding Issue, The Brooklyn Rail, Literary Mama, The Rumpus*, and others. She and her husband split their time between Brooklyn, the Catskills, and the West coast where their son and other dear ones live.

Callista Buchen is the author of the full-length collection *Look Look Look* (forthcoming from Black Lawrence Press) and the chapbooks *The Bloody Planet* (Black Lawrence Press) and *Double-Mouthed* (dancing girl press). Her work appears in *Harpur Palate, Puerto del Sol, Fourteen Hills,* and many other journals, and she is the winner of the Langston Hughes Award and DIAGRAM's essay contest.

Jody Burke-Kaiser was born barefoot in the Appalachian foothills to a family long steeped in storytelling and sarcasm. She has a MA in literature from Boston College and an MSN in midwifery from Marquette University. She is a Pushcart Prize nominee, and her work has appeared in *Panoply, The Louisville Review, RHINO, Gingerbread House, After Hours, BrainChild*, and *Pirene's Fountain*. She lives in Chicago with her husband and half-feral children.

Wendy Cannella's poetry has appeared in *Mid-American Review, Painted Bride Quarterly*, and *Salamander,* with new work forthcoming in *Crab Creek Review* and *Balancing Act 2* (Littoral Books). Her essay "Angels and Terrorists" is featured in *The Room and the World: Essays on the Poet Stephen Dunn* from Syracuse University Press. She serves as co-chair on the board of directors of the Portsmouth Poet Laureate Project and lives in York, Maine.

Jennifer Case is the author of *Sawbill: A Search for Place* (University of New Mexico Press, 2018). Her essays have appeared in journals such as *Orion, Michigan Quarterly Review, Literary Mama, Fourth River, Sycamore Review*, and *Zone 3*. She teaches at the University of Central Arkansas and serves as the Assistant Nonfiction Editor of *Terrain.org*. You can find her at www.jenniferlcase.com.

Breena Clarke is the author of three novels, most recently *Angels Make Their Hope Here*, set in 19th century New Jersey. Her debut novel, *River, Cross My Heart*, was an Oprah Book Club selection. Her critically reviewed second novel, *Stand The Storm,* was named 200 Best of 2008. Her short fiction has appeared in *Kweli Journal, Stonecoast Review, Nervous Breakdown, Mom Egg Review, The Drabble*, and *Catapult*. She is on the fiction faculty of Stonecoast MFA in Creative Writing.

Poet and essayist **Heidi Czerwiec** is the author of the poetry collection *Conjoining* and of the forthcoming lyric essay collection *Fluid States*, selected by Dinty W. Moore as winner of Pleiades Press 2018 Robert C. Jones Prize for Short Prose. She lives in Minneapolis, where she is an editor for *Assay: A Journal of Nonfiction Studies* and for *Poetry City*, and mentors with the Minnesota Prison Writing Workshop. Visit her at heidiczerwiec.com.

Teri Ellen Cross Davis is the author of *Haint* (Gival Press, 2016), winner of the 2017 Ohioana Book Award for Poetry. She is a Cave Canem fellow and a member of the Black Ladies Brunch Collective. Her work has been published in many anthologies and journals. She lives in Maryland with her husband, poet Hayes Davis, and their two children.

Lisa DeSiro is the author of *Labor* (Nixes Mate, 2018) and *Grief Dreams* (White Knuckle Press, 2017). Her poetry is featured in various anthologies and journals and has been set to music by several composers. Along with her job as Production & Editorial Assistant for *C.P.E. Bach: The Complete Works,* Lisa is an assistant editor for Indolent Books and a freelance accompanist. Read more about her at thepoetpianist. com.

Carol Dorf has two chapbooks, *Some Years Ask,* (Moria Press) and *Theory Headed Dragon,* (Finishing Line Press). Her poetry appears in *Bodega, E-ratio, Great Weather For Media, About Place, Glint, Slipstream, Mom Egg Review, Sin Fronteras, Surreal Poetics, The Journal of Humanistic Mathematics, Scientific American,* and *Maintenant.* She is poetry editor of *Talking Writing* and teaches math in Berkeley. She is interested in the intersections between disability, science and parenting.

Iris Jamahl Dunkle was the 2017-2018 Poet Laureate of Sonoma County, CA. Her poetry collections include *Interrupted Geographies* (2017), *There's a Ghost in this Machine of Air* (2015) and *Gold Passage* (2013). Her biography on Charmian Kitteridge London, Jack London's wife, will be published by University of Oklahoma Press in Spring 2020. Dunkle teaches at Napa Valley College and is the Poetry Director of the Napa Valley Writers' Conference.

Suzanne Edison MA, MFA. Suzanne's recent chapbook, *The Body Lives Its Undoing,* was published by Benaroya Research Institute. Poetry can be found in: *Canadian Medical Association Journal, Michigan Quarterly Review, HEAL, Isacoustic, Persimmon Tree, JAMA, SWWIM, Intima: A Journal of Narrative Medicine, The Ekphrastic Review,* and in the anthologies *Face to Face: Women Writers on Faith, Mysticism and Awakening* and *The Healing Art of Writing.* She lives in Seattle and teaches at Richard Hugo House.

Alexis Rhone Fancher is published in *Best American Poetry 2016, Rattle, Hobart, Verse Daily, Plume, Tinderbox, Cleaver,* and elsewhere. Her books include: *How I Lost My Virginity to Michael Cohen…, State of Grace: The Joshua Elegies, Enter Here,* and *Junkie Wife.* Her photographs are published worldwide, including the covers of *Witness, Heyday,* and *Pithead Chapel,* and spreads in *River Styx* and *Chiron Review.* A multiple Pushcart Prize nominee, Alexis is poetry editor of *Cultural Weekly.*

Kelly Fordon's work has appeared in various journals. Her novel-in-stories, *Garden for the Blind,* was chosen as a Michigan Notable Book, an Indiefab Finalist and a Midwest Book Award Finalist, among others. She is the author of three award-winning poetry chapbooks. Her first full-length poetry collection will be published by Kattywompus Press in 2019. www.kellyfordon.com

Kate Hanson Foster's first book of poems, *Mid Drift,* was published by Loom Press and was a finalist for the Massachusetts Center for the Book Award in 2011. Her work has appeared in *Comstock Review, Harpur Palate, Poet Lore, Salamander, Tupelo Quarterly, FIVE:2:ONE Magazine* and elsewhere. She was recently awarded the NEA Parent Fellowship through the Vermont Studio Center.

Sarah Freligh is the author of *Sad Math,* winner of the 2014 Moon City Press Poetry Prize and the 2015 Whirling Prize from the University of Indianapolis. Her fiction and poetry have appeared in *Sun Magazine, SmokeLong Quarterly, Cincinnati Review* and in the anthology *New Microfiction: Exceptionally Short Stories* (W.W. Norton, 2018). She was the recipient of a poetry fellowship from the National Endowment for the Arts in 2009.

Jen Stewart Fueston lives in Longmont, Colorado. Her poem in this issue of *MER* is included in her recently published second chapbook, *Latch*, from River Glass Books, which explores infertility, nursing, and the early days of motherhood. Her poems have appeared most recently *in Ruminate, Rock & Sling* and *The St. Katherine Review*, and have been nominated for a Pushcart Prize. She has taught writing at the University of Colorado, Boulder, as well as internationally in Hungary, Turkey, and Lithuania.

Robbie Gamble's poems have appeared in *Scoundrel Time, Solstice, Slipstream, RHINO* and *Poet Lore*. He was the winner of the 2017 Carve Poetry prize. He works as a nurse practitioner caring for homeless people in Boston, Massachusetts.

Alisa A. Gaston's work has appeared in *Hotel Amerika, The Tishman Review, Brain Child, The Sun, The Montreal Review*, and other publications. She spent several years writing for the U.S. Antarctic Program, has taught creative writing to youth at Denver's Lighthouse Writers, and has volunteered as a creative writing workshop facilitator for the Boys and Girls Club and Urban Peak Teen Shelter. Alisa lives in Colorado with her husband, daughter, two Weimaraners, and a cat. www.alisagaston.com

Sherine Gilmour graduated with an MFA in Poetry from New York University. She was nominated for a Pushcart Prize, and her poems have appeared or are forthcoming in *American Journal of Poetry, River Styx, So To Speak, Tinderbox,* and other publications.

Heather Haldeman lives in Pasadena, California. Her work has been published in T*he Christian Science Monitor, Chicken Soup for the Soul, From Freckles to Wrinkles, Grandmother Earth, Mom Egg Review* and numerous online journals. She has received first, second and third prizes for her essays. She has just completed a memoir about growing up in wealth and ruin in Los Angeles during the Mad Men era. Visit her blog at Heatherhaldeman.blogspot.com.

James Hoch's poems have appeared in *The New Republic, Washington Post, Slate, Chronicle Review of Higher Education, American Poetry Review, New England Review, Kenyon Review, Tin House, Ploughshares, Virginia Quarterly Review* and many other magazines. His books are *A Parade of Hands* and *Miscreants*. He has received fellowships from the NEA, Bread Loaf and Sewanee Writers Conferences, St Albans School for Boys, Summer Literary Seminars. Currently, he is Professor of Creative Writing at Ramapo College of New Jersey and Guest Faculty at Sarah Lawrence.

Vicki Iorio is the author of *Poems from the Dirty Couch* (Local Gems Press) and the chapbooks *Send Me a Letter* (dancinggirlpress) and *Something Fishy* (Finishing Line Press). Her poetry has appeared in numerous print and on-line journals, including *The Painted Bride Quarterly, Rattle, Poets Respond* online, and *The Fem Lit Magazine.*

Christine Jones is founder/editor of poems2go, a public poetry project. Her most recent poetry can be found or is forthcoming in *32 poems, Salamander, Crab Creek Review, Cimarron Review, Naugatuck Review, Lily Poetry Review,* and others. She and her husband can be found on the shores of Cape Cod surfing or swimming in matching shark-mitigating wet suits.

Crystal Karlberg teaches middle school in Massachusetts. Her poems have been published in *The Compassion Anyhology, Ekphrastic Review,* and *Soundings East.* Her prose has been published in *Scary Mommy.*

Tina Kelley's third poetry collection, *Abloom and Awry*, came out in 2017 from CavanKerry Press, joining *Precise* and *The Gospel of Galore*, which won a 2003 Washington State Book Award. *Ardor* won the 2017 Jacar Press chapbook competition. A former New York Times reporter, she shared in a staff Pulitzer for 9/11 coverage and co-authored *Almost Home: Helping Kids Move from Homelessness to Hope.* She lives in New Jersey with her husband and two children.

Dr. Juanita Kirton earned an MFA from Goddard College. Member of Women Who Write, Inc. and Women Reading Aloud workshop series. Is on editorial staff for *Clockhouse Literary Journal.* Recently published in *Persimmon Tree, Narrative, Stone Canoe, Rat's Ass Online Journal, Veterans Voices Magazine* and *Nasty Women Poets Anthology.* Dr. Kirton is a Compliance Advisor, PA Department of Education, US Army Veteran. Resides with her spouse in Northeast PA. Besides writing, motorcycling is her other passion.

Cyn Kitchen teaches creative writing and literature at Knox College. Her book *Ten Tongues* was published in 2010. She also has work out in the world at *Still, Spry, Stirring* and *vox poetica,* among other places. Cyn makes her home in Forgottonia, a downstate region on the Illinois prairie.

Andrei Konchalovsky collaborated on screenplays with budding legend Andrei Tarkovsky before cementing his own place in Soviet cinema, then leaving Moscow, at no small scandal, for Hollywood, where he also would eventually leave his mark. In the 1990s, he returned to Russia, continuing to direct movies, plays and opera. In 2014 and 2016, he was named best director at the Venice International Film Festival for, respectively, "The Postman's White Nights" and "Paradise."

Lavinia Kumar's books are *The Celtic Fisherman's Wife: A Druid Life* (2017) and *The Skin and Under* (Word Tech, 2015). Her chapbooks are *Let There be Color* (Lives You Touch Publications, 2016), *Rivers of Saris* (Main Street Rag, 2013), and *Beauty. Salon. Art* to be published by Desert Willow Press, 2019. Her poems have appeared in US, UK and Irish publications. Her website is laviniakumar.org.

Xiaoly Li is a poet, photographer and former computer engineer who lives in Massachusetts. Her poetry is forthcoming or has recently appeared in *RHINO Poetry, The Mantle, Big Windows Review, Up the River, The Writers Next Door: An Anthology of Poetry and Prose, J Journal* and many other journals. Xiaoly received her Ph.D. in electrical engineering in America and a Master's in computer science and engineering in China.

Judith Lichtendorf writes fiction and memoir. She lives in Manhattan. She's studied with some great writers, among them Lore Segal, Rick Moody, and Teddy Wayne. She believes the sun rises each morning to honor the perfection of her two grandchildren, Amira and Max.

Tsaurah Litzky, a longtime trendsetter in the margins, writes poetry, fiction, creative prose, plays, erotica and commentary. Her poetry publications include *Baby On The Water* (Long Shot Press) and *Cleaning The Duck* (Bowery Books) and fourteen poetry chapbooks, most recently, *Full Lotus: Poems About Yoga* (NightBallet Press). Her books include the novella, *The Motion Of The Ocean* , published by Simon and Schuster and *Flasher: A Memoir,* published by Unbearables /Autonomedia in 2018.

Bryon MacWilliams is an American writer and translator who was a Moscow-based correspondent, covering the territories of the former Soviet Union for nearly twelve years. He is author of the books *With Light Steam* and *The Girl in the Haystack.* His journalism, essays, poetry, and translations have appeared in publications big and small, including: *The New York Times, The Chronicle of Higher Education, The Literary Review, B O D Y, Solstice,* and *Nature.*

Tasslyn Magnusson received her MFA in Creative Writing for Children and Young Adults at Hamline University in Saint Paul, MN. Her poems have been published in *Room Magazine* and *Red Weather Online.* Her chapbook, *Defining,* is forthcoming from dancing girl press. She lives with her husband, two kids, and two dogs in Prescott, Wisconsin.

April Matisz is a mother-artist based in Lethbridge, Alberta. Matisz's practice spans drawing, printmaking, and painting. Her work draws on her knowledge of the sciences, exploring ecology, landscape, and phenomenology. Presently, she investigates aspects of motherhood: the mother's ambivalence, the suppression of her identity, her relationship to her children, and cultural narratives surrounding motherhood. The influence of the environment on the self and the intersections of biology and culture are themes found throughout her work.

Caitlin Grace McDonnell was a New York Times Poetry Fellow at NYU, where she received her MFA. She has published a chapbook, *Dreaming the Tree* (belladonna books, 2003) and a book, *Looking for Small Animals* (Nauset Press, 2012). Her poems, essays and book reviews have appeared in numerous print and online publications, including *Salon, Washington Square, Chronogram* and more. She teaches writing in Brooklyn, NY, where she lives with daughter, Kaya Hope.

Megan Merchant is an Editor at *Comstock Review*. Her most recent book, *Grief Flowers* (Glass Lyre Press) is currently out in the world. You can find her work at meganmerchant.wix.com/poet.

MaryAnn L. Miller's most recent book of poems is *Cures for Hysteria* (Finishing Line Press, 2018.) She has been twice nominated for a Pushcart Prize. Her work has been published in *Ovunque Siamo, Stillwater Review, Wordgathering, Kaleidoscope, International Review of African American Art* and others. Her poem "Canaletto Validates My Grandmother" won Honorable Mention in the *Passager* poetry contest for 2018. She publishes artists' books pairing poets and visual artists through her www.luciapress.com.

Kathleen Mitchell-Askar holds degrees from UCLA and California State University, Northridge. Her work has appeared in, or is forthcoming from, *DIAGRAM, Rust+Moth, SWWIM Everyday,* and *Whale Road Review*. She lives, works, and writes in Sacramento.

Elizabeth Newdom teaches composition and literature courses at a community college in Frederick, MD. Her work has appeared in *The Manifest-Station, Mothers Always Write, Mutha Magazine,* and *The Good Men Project*, among others. Elizabeth also writes about the beauty and grit of traveling to the moon and back on her blog, The Astronaut Wife.

Rebecca Hart Olander's poetry has appeared recently in *Ilanot Review, Plath Poetry Project,* and *Solstice*, and collaborative work made with Elizabeth Paul has been published in *They Said: A Multi-Genre Anthology of Contemporary Collaborative Writing* (BLP) and online at *Duende*. Rebecca won the 2013 Women's National Book Association poetry contest. She lives in Western Massachusetts, where she teaches writing at Westfield State University and is the editor/director of Perugia Press. Find her @rholanderpoet and rebeccahartolander.com.

Devin Overman is an author and screenwriter whose fiction has appeared in *Soft Cartel* and *NILVX*. Her screenplay, "Falling Into the Sound," has been optioned by Little Studio Films. She lives in Dallas with her son Stark who might be part cat.

eve packer is a Bronx-born poet/performer/actress, appearing widely with dance, poetry, performance, music, theatre. NEH, NYSCA, NYFA awards. Downtown Poet of the Year awards. Numerous publications. Three poetry books (Fly by Night Press); five poetry/jazz CD's. Teaches at WCC. Mom, Grandmom, lives downtown, swims daily.

Carla Panciera has published two collections of poetry: *One of the Cimalores* (Cider Press) and *No Day, No Dusk, No Love* (Bordighera). Her collection of short stories, *Bewildered*, received AWP's 2013 Grace Paley Short Fiction Award. Her work has appeared in several journals, including *Poetry, The New England Review, Nimrod, The Chattahoochee Review, Painted Bride,* and *Carolina Quarterly*. Carla lives in Rowley, MA, with her husband and three daughters.

Lynn Patmalnee's work has appeared in *The Berkeley Poetry Review, BigCityLit* and *Neon*, among others. A born and bred Jersey Girl, she's living her lifelong dream of having a Tilt-A-Whirl in her backyard in Keansburg. As Lynn Crystal, she is a DJ on WFDU FM.

Dayna Patterson's creative work has appeared recently in *Hotel Amerika, So to Speak, Western Humanities Review,* and *Zone 3*. She is a former managing editor of *Bellingham Review,* founding editor-in-chief of *Psaltery & Lyre,* and poetry editor for *Exponent II Magazine.* She is a co-editor of *Dove Song: Heavenly Mother in Mormon Poetry* (Peculiar Pages, 2018). Connect with her at: daynapatterson.com.

Robert Perron lives and writes in New Hampshire and New York City. Past life includes high-tech and military service, along with marriage and children. His stories have appeared in *The Manchester Review, Sweet Tree Review, STORGY Magazine, Adelaide Literary Magazine, The Fictional Café*, and other journals. Visit his website at https://robertperron.com.

Tzynya L. Pinchback (tzynyapinchback.com) is author of the chapbook *How to Make Pink Confetti* (dancing girl press, 2012). Poems and essays from her current manuscript, "Tulle," appear in *The American Poetry Journal, the Aurorean, Midnight & Indigo, Rhythm of the Bones,* and *Up the Staircase Quarterly.* She writes software manuals and poetry from a small cottage in New England next to the sea.

Anne Elezabeth Pluto grew up in Brooklyn, way before it was cool. She is a Professor at Lesley University in Cambridge, MA, and the Artistic Director of the Oxford Street Players. She is one of the founders and editors at *Nixes Mate Review / Nixes Mate Books.* She has three chapbooks, *The Frog Princess,* (White Pine Press, 1985), *Benign Protection*, (Cervena Barva Press, 2016), and *Lubbock Electric,* (Nixes Mate Books, 2018).

Kyle Potvin's chapbook, *Sound Travels on Water* (Finishing Line Press), won the 2014 Jean Pedrick Chapbook Award. She is a two-time finalist for the Howard Nemerov Sonnet Award. Her poems have appeared in *Bellevue Literary Review, Crab Creek Review, The New York Times, The Huffington Post, Measure, JAMA,* and others. She is an advisor to Frost Farm Poetry in Derry, NH, and helps produce the New Hampshire Poetry Festival.

Renuka Raghavan's previous work has been featured in *Boston Literary Magazine, Chicago Literati, Nixes Mate Review, Gravel Literary Magazine,* and elsewhere. She is the author of *Out of the Blue,* a collection of short fiction and poetry. Renuka serves as the fiction book reviewer at Červená Barva Press, and is a co-founder of the Poetry Sisters Collective. Visit her at www.renukaraghavan.com.

Lois Roma-Deeley's fourth collection of poems, *The Short List of Certainties*, is the Jacopone da Todi Book Prize winner (2017). She is the author of three previous collections of poetry: *Rules of Hunger, northSight* and *High Notes,* a Paterson Poetry Prize Finalist. Her poetry is featured in numerous anthologies and journals. Currently, she serves as Associate Editor of the international poetry journal *Presence.* www.loisroma-deeley.com

Rosemary Royston, author of *Splitting the Soil* (Finishing Line Press, 2014), resides in northeast Georgia with her family. Her poetry has been published in journals such as *Appalachian Heritage, Split Rock Review, Southern Poetry Review, KUDZU, Town Creek Review,* and **82 Review.* She's the VP for Planning and Special Projects at Young Harris College, where she teaches the occasional creative writing course.

Margie Shaheed was a community poet, writer and teaching artist and the author of seven books of poetry and prose, including *Playground* (Hidden Charm Press) and *Onomatopoeia, Mosaic,* and *Throwback Thursdays* (all from Nightballet Press). Her "Playground" stories can be found at www.timbooktu.com. Margie Shaheed passed away in 2018.

Neil Silberblatt's poems have appeared in numerous journals and anthologies, including *Poetica Magazine, the Aurorean, Ibbetson Street Press, Naugatuck River Review, Muddy River Poetry Review*, and *Nixes Mate Review*. He has published two poetry collections: *So Far, So Good* (2012) and *Present Tense* (2013), and has been nominated for a Pushcart Prize. His most recent poetry book, *Past Imperfect* (Nixes Mate Books, 2018), was recently nominated for the Massachusetts Book Award.

Jill Slaymaker lives and works in Hell's Kitchen, Manhattan. Her art work has been exhibited at the Tate Modern, London; Dabawenyo Museum, Philippines; Blum Helman, New York; Kustera Projects, New York; and Pierogi, New York; with recent solo exhibitions at Port Authority, New York City; The Nabi Museum of the Arts in New Jersey; and The Davis Mini-Museum of Contemporary Art in Barcelona. She was nominated for a 2018 Winter Workspace at Wave Hill and awarded a grant from the Hell's Kitchen Foundation. She had an art residency at La Macina di San Cresci in Tuscany, Italy. Her work is in numerous public collections, including The Museum of Modern Art, New York and the Whitney Museum of American Art, New York. https://www.jillslaymaker.com.

Hali F. Sofala-Jones is a Samoan American teacher and writer. She holds an MFA in Poetry from the University of Wisconsin, Madison, and a Ph.D. in English from the University of Nebraska, Lincoln. Her poetry appears in *Nimrod International Journal, The Bitter Oleander, CALYX, Blue Mesa Review, The Missouri Review, The Samoan Observer,* and elsewhere. Her debut collection of poetry, *AFAKASI | HALF-CASTE* is forthcoming in 2019 from Sundress Publications.

Linda Spolidoro is a writer, poet, melancholic, and dedicated yogi. After years of questionable decision making, she found the yogic path, gave up smoking, drinking, swearing, and sex. Well, smoking. Linda runs a monthly Poetry Open Mic in Beverly, Massachusetts called The Cellar, has been published in several small journals, including *Popshot Magazine, The Clockwise Cat, American Chordata, Naked Bruce Review,* and *Soundings East*. Her first collection is forthcoming from YesNo Press in Salem.

Autumn Stephens is a writer, editor, and teacher. The author of the *Wild Women* book series and editor of two anthologies of women's first-person essays, she teaches private writing classes and leads writing groups for cancer survivors. Autumn is the former co-editor of the *East Bay Monthly* and a contributing editor to *Talking Writing*. She lives in a near-empty nest in Berkeley, CA.

Alison Stone has published four full-length collections, *Dazzle* (Jacar Press, 2018), *Ordinary Magic* (NYQ Books, 2016), *Dangerous Enough* (Presa Pressk, 2014), and *They Sing at Midnight*, which won the 2003 Many Mountains Moving Poetry Award, as well as three chapbooks. *Masterplan*, a book of collaborative poems with Eric Greinke, is due out in 2018. Her poems have appeared in *The Paris Review, Poetry, Ploughshares, Barrow Street, Poet Lore,* and many other journals and anthologies. She has been awarded *Poetry's* Frederick Bock Prize and *New York Quarterly's* Madeline Sadin Award. www.stonepoetry.org; www.stonetarot.com.

Judy Swann is a poet and essayist whose work has been published in many venues both in print and online. Her work includes a book of poetry, *Fool* (Kelsay Books, 2019), a book of letters, *We Are All Well: The Letters of Nora Hall* (YoungBros, 2016) and a book of essays on the cartoon superhero *Stickman* (John Young, 2019). She lives in Ithaca, NY.

Cammy Thomas has published two collections of poems with Four Way Books: *Inscriptions* (2014) and *Cathedral of Wish*, which received the 2006 Norma Farber First Book Award from the Poetry Society of America. Her poems are forthcoming or have recently appeared in *Slipstream, Moon City Review, The Summerset Review, The Tampa Review,* and *The Missouri Review*. A fellowship from the Ragdale Foundation helped her complete *Inscriptions*. Cammy lives in Lexington, Massachusetts.

Sharon Tracey is a writer and editor and author of the poetry collection, *What I Remember Most Is Everything* (ALL CAPS PUBLISHING, 2017). Her poems have appeared in *Common Ground Review, Light: A Journal of Photography and Poetry, Ekphrasis, Naugatuck River Review* and elsewhere. Art and nature are recurring themes in her work. She lives in Amherst, Massachusetts.

Pramila Venkateswaran, poet laureate of Suffolk County and co-director of Matwaala: South Asian Diaspora Poetry Festival, is the author of *Thirtha, Behind Dark Waters, Draw Me Inmost, Trace, Thirteen Days to Let Go, Slow Ripening, The Singer of Alleppey.* An award-winning poet, she teaches English and Women's Studies at SUNY Nassau.

Nancy Vona writes creative non-fiction, poetry, and children's literature. Her writing has been published in *Mom Egg Review, Literary Mama, Spillway,* and *Naugatuck River Review.* She lives in Massachusetts with her family, rescued dogs, and honeybees. One more thing: the world is round, evolution happens, and climate change is real.

Sara Moore Wagner is the author of the chapbook *Hooked Through* (Five Oaks Press, 2017). Her poetry has appeared or is forthcoming in many journals, including *Western Humanities Review, Gulf Stream,* and *Gigantic Sequins,* among others. She has been nominated for a Pushcart prize and is a 2018 Best of the Net nominee. She is a mother of three. Find her at www.saramoorewagner.com.

Ann E. Wallace writes of life with illness, motherhood, and other everyday realities. Her poetry collection *Counting by Sevens* is forthcoming from Main Street Rag this summer, and her published work, featured in journals such as *Wordgathering, The Literary Nest, Rogue Agent, Mothers Always Write,* and *Juniper,* can be found on her website AnnWallacePhD.com. She lives in Jersey City, NJ and is on Twitter @annwlace409.

Kristy Webster is the author of *The Gift of an Imaginary Girl: Coco and Other Stories.* She earned her MFA from Pacific Lutheran University and a M.I.T. from Heritage University. Her work has appeared in online journals such as *Lunch Ticket, Pithead Chapel, The Feminist Wire, Shark Reef Literary Magazine, Pacifica Literary Review, The Molotov Cocktail, Connotation Press,* as well as in the anthology *Two Countries,* published by Red Hen Press.

Given the name Many Trails Many Roads Woman by the medicine man of her Northern Cheyenne tribe, **Sheree Winslow** embraces a life of wander and wonder. Her work has been published in *Midway Journal, *82 Review,* and *Beecher's,* among others. Winner of the 2018 Submittable.com Eliza So Fellowship, Sheree is completing a memoir about recovery from food addiction and a book of travel reflections. She received an MFA from Vermont College of Fine Arts.

Megan Wynne is a photographer and multi-media artist based in Chesapeake, Virginia. Her work addresses issues of emotional interdependence and intimacy, with a focus on the subject of motherhood. For the past five years she has worked with her children in collaborative scenarios that result in unpredictable and spontaneous interactions with them. The resulting work explores maternal identity and vulnerability, uncertainty, and the underlying and shifting dynamics of power in the mother-child relationship.

Jane Yolen will have published over 376 books by the end of 2018. She has worked in almost every genre possible. Her books include several NY Times bestselling children's picture books, prize-winning short stories, and poems. Six colleges and universities have given her honorary doctorates. She was the first writer to win the New England Public Radio's Arts & Humanities award. She's mother of three (all in the book business) and grandmother of six.

MOM EGG REVIEW

Mom Egg Review Issues Available

Vol. 16 "Play and Work"	2018, Paper, 118 pp. $18
Vol. 15	2017 Paper, 123 pp. $18
Vol. 14 "Change"	2016 Paper, 128 pp. $18
Vol. 13 "Compassionate Action"	2015 Paper, 154 pp. $18
Vol. 12	2014 Paper, 150 pp. $18
Vol. 11 "Mother Tongue"	2013 Paper, 125 pp. $18
Vol. 10 "The Body"	2012 Paper, 120 pp. $18
Vol. 9	2011 Paper, 120 pp. $18
Vol. 8 "Lessons"	2010 Paper, 120 pp. $18
Vol. 7	2009 Paper, 124 pp. $18

*Plus US shipping $3.50 for the first book, $1.00 for each additional book.

Subscribe to *MER*

US shipping is free for subscription copies!

One year $18
Two years $36

Order on the web at
www.momeggreview.com (Click "Shop")

or mail your order with a check to

Mom Egg Review
Half-Shell Press
PO Box 9037
Bardonia, NY 10954

Contact: info@themomegg.com

Email info@themomegg.com for info about discounts for quantity purchases and for classroom use, or for out-of-country shipping.